ZEN

ZEN STYLE

balance and simplicity for your home

with special photography by **Peter Aprahamian**

WARD LOCK
LONDON

published in association with

Livingetc

THE MODERN HOME & LIFESTYLE MAGAZINE

Jane Tidbury

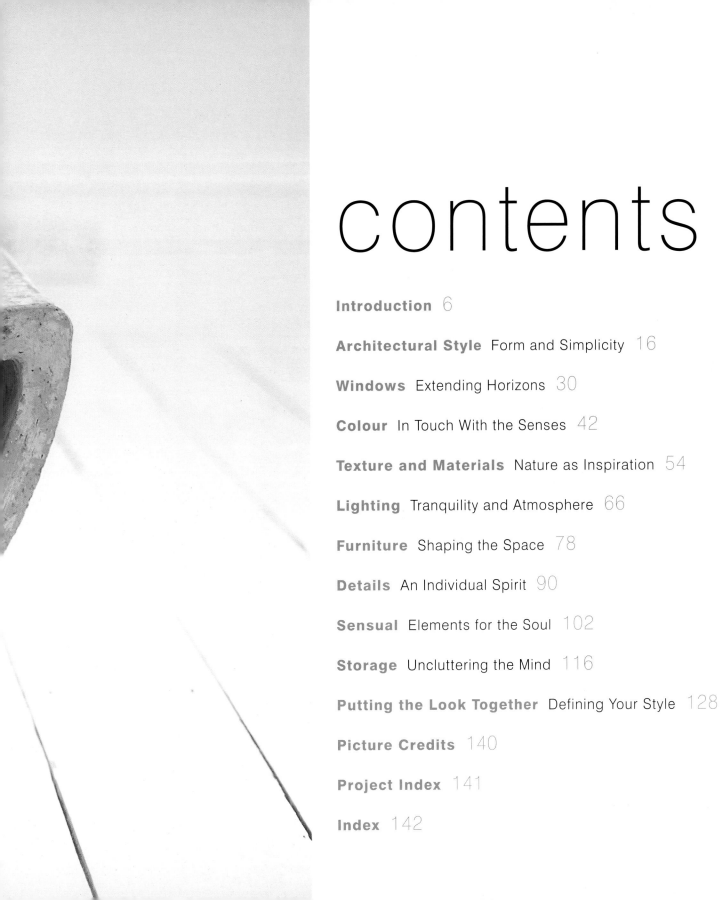

contents

introduction

Abide in some place endlessly spacious,
clear of trees, hills, habitations.
Thence comes the end of mind pressures.

Ancient Sanskrit text

What is Zen?

Most of us have at one time stood on a beach and been completely captivated by the sights and sounds of the sea, carried away to the point where all other thoughts seem to disappear. And perhaps, lost in the sensations of our surroundings, out of nowhere it seems, we have suddenly been struck by the beauty of a fleeting detail – a ripple of sunlight cutting through the water, the patterns of waves tumbling across the sand. We might have seen it all before, but in that briefest of moments we experience it with a new and fresh eye, as though we were seeing it for the very first time – you might say we have experienced a touch of Zen.

In the philosophical sense, a Zen teacher would probably say there is no answer to the question: What is Zen? Zen is an approach to life, a way of being, rather than a philosophy or set doctrine. It is more a personal journey of discovery which aims to free the mind so that a greater level of awareness – both of ourselves and the world around us – can be achieved. Since each journey is unique, Zen has no rules or set paths to follow. Instead, there are merely guidelines by which a person is encouraged to find and follow their own course.

Although we tend to associate Zen with the idea of deep meditation and enlightenment (both are interpretations of the meaning of the word Zen), in fact the true spirit of Zen is much more accessible.

For the central focus of Zen (the word and the teachings) concerns itself with less grandiose ideals. It is rooted in the real world and the idea that our connection with even the most ordinary of day-to-day things can provide an opportunity for insight and understanding. That even in the most mundane of tasks we can suddenly be struck by a 'flash of awareness' or new way of seeing, known as Satori.

In the bigger picture, Satori is seen as the key to opening doors on the path of our Zen journey, but it is also important in its own right. Like our ripples of light in the sea, Satori is not something that can be described in words, it is something we feel intuitively without definition. But the experience of it can bring joy, a feeling of well-being, peacefulness, calm and contentment. And because of all this, it enriches us and brings a sense of balance and perspective to our lives.

The route to Satori (and possibly beyond) is through a mind that is open. If we approach the world with cluttered thoughts, preconceptions, or expectations, then we see and experience only what we expect. How do we clear our minds? Typically we might think of the dedicated monk spending hours in meditation, but that is not the only way of Zen. Even the simple act of relaxation, closing our eyes and allowing our thoughts to wander, is in itself an opening of the mind, so that when we open them again we see the world afresh.

The Zen home

If Zen is a new way of seeing, then the Zen home is about changing the way we think about our home and our relationship to it. Most of us would think of the home as a sanctuary – a place to which we retreat at the end of the day. But if our home is to be a true sanctuary, then it has to be a place where we can experience new things, where we can rediscover aspects forgotten in the rush of life, and where we can feel balanced and calm.

Zen style is not a fashion statement. Nor is it about creating a Zen meditation space or a Japanese inspired interior – although of course, it could incorporate both or either of these aspects. Zen style is about self-expression – creating a space that suits each of us as an individual, allowing us to feel positive and refreshed when we are there.

Rather than focusing on fussy decorative treatments, the Zen approach is to think first about the fundamental aspects of the home: what we want from it; how the space can be utilized to its full potential; the purpose and position of every item we have, from the largest piece of furniture to the smallest detail.

If, by clearing our mind we become more receptive, then by clearing our living space we can assume that we will become more finely tuned to our needs and the potential of our home. The initial aim of the Zen home is to free the space of confusion and distractions and create a simplified interior. Into this we can add dimensions such as colour, texture, shape and scent to invigorate us. For the Zen home is not a sterile environment – one set by restrictions – but one that comes alive with the inclusion of natural objects, serene colour and elegant shapes.

In essence, Zen style represents a modest approach to home decorating. When the superfluous details are removed, we are able to have a more intimate relationship with what is left. While there is an emphasis on the application and appreciation of natural materials in the Zen home, which rekindle our connection with the natural world, there is always room for excellent designs in man-made materials. Design decisions should be rooted in an awareness of the environment and our duty towards it, and this book suggests a more considered approach to furniture, paints and materials. It recommends responsible consumerism, respect for resources, re-cycling where necessary and using natural alternatives where possible.

Whether we are able to completely rethink the place in which we live, change one room or simply adopt a shift in attitude, small or large steps, we can all do something to bring a touch of Zen into our homes. And it begins with the consideration of a few essential elements discussed on the following pages.

Elements
of Zen

Every space can be adapted
to feel more open and calm, to
become a place where we can
find true relaxation, balance and
peace of mind. For the essence
of the Zen home is found not so
much in the choices we make
but in the thinking behind those
choices and in the essential
elements that are part and
parcel of any home – the form
and structure, the light, the
furnishings and the ordinary
possessions of the everyday.

space
freedom for the spirit

We break down the confines of our home with
clean lines and streamlined simplicity to
encourage a sense of openness. In this way,
our surroundings become more fluid and
free-flowing..

light
freshness and vitality

A room flooded with daylight seems to expand the proportions of a space and diffuse the boundaries between rooms. We can relax in a room that is filled with warm light and feel instantly invigorated and energized.

natural
connecting with the spirit of life

The colours and patterns
of natural objects balance
the streamlined surround-
ings and serve to remind
us of the importance,
and the beauty, of the
natural world.

simplicity
uncluttering the mind and soothing the soul

A pared-down style, with
strong clean lines, minimal
detailing and cool colours,
provides a calm setting.

texture
the experience of touch

A medley of different textures stimulates the senses making the home not just a thing of beauty to be admired by sight from a distance, but something we can feel connected to through the experience of touch.

purity

a new way of seeing

When we see something in isolation, we see it without distraction. We see it more intensely and more clearly. The colour of a flower, the movement of water, the outline of an object – in their purest form, we can see beyond the obvious.

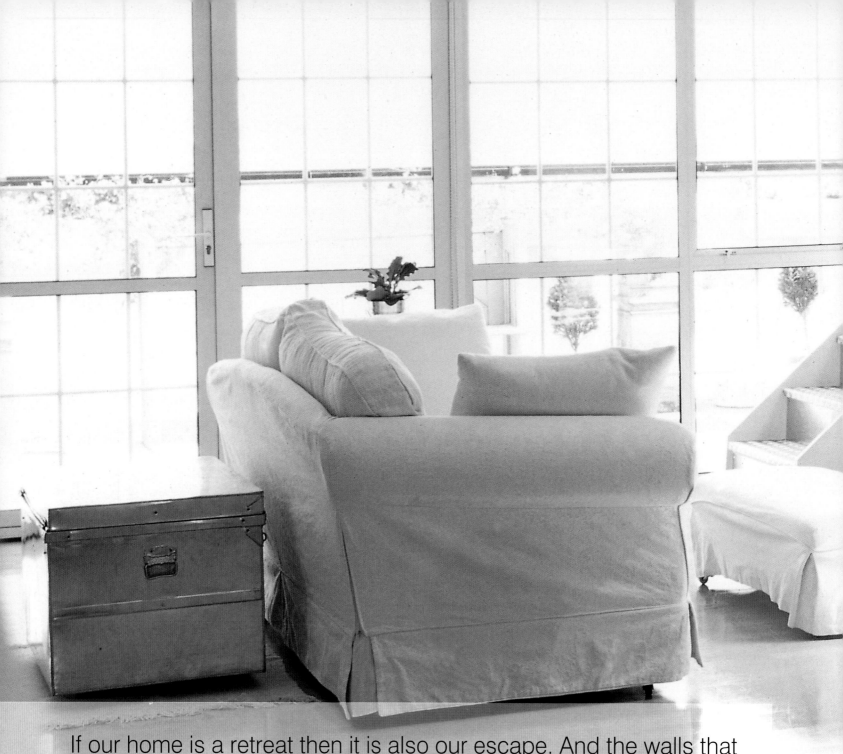

If our home is a retreat then it is also our escape. And the walls that cocoon us from the outside world have the potential to become our gateway to freedom.

architectural style
form and simplicity

When we think about any given room in our home, it is invariably the space and atmosphere that we remember most clearly. A room full of light with airy qualities can suddenly lift the spirit, making us feel calm as well as invigorated. And yet, inspite of this, we still tend to define a room by the colours, the fabrics, and the style of furniture and accessories. Often, these decorative layers mask the inherent quality and atmosphere of a room. Decorative details demand our attention, directing our mind rather than releasing it. To create a home that is free of clutter, we need to peel away these extraneous layers to reveal the internal structure – the division of rooms and their relation to each other. The Zen home strives to achieve a fluid environment in which the simplicity and sophistication of the architectural style unifies the whole interior, exaggerating the impression of space and light.

To provide room for us to move and breathe, our surroundings need to be understated and without imposition. We need to feel free of our environment rather than controlled by it. A sense of space is the most important element and all other considerations feed into this. If we were to remove the walls of our home we would have an interior landscape that is fluid and limitless. Structurally of course, it is not practical to remove every wall, but this is in a sense the aim of the Zen home – to create a place that feels open, and without boundaries (or direction), a place where we no longer feel confined by the structure.

Setting the spirit free

For the eye and mind to flow freely through the Zen home, the architectural style must be without distractions. Clean lines, pale colours,

restrained repeat patterns, and smooth, uninterrupted walls and floors all help to lead the eye onwards, giving the home a sense of space. Strong shapes and outlines, and the use of symmetry bring a sense of order and balance to the architectural style. In this way, walls and floors do not jostle for attention, but recede from the eye, and the feeling of space and light intensifies.

Doorways without decorative surroundings or with the door removed, for example, frame the entrance of a room so that the eye does not dwell on the door frame but moves naturally into the room beyond. Similarly, clean outlines around a series of interior doorways seem to meld with the walls and our vision is carried forward to the textures and colours of the next space and then the space after that.

LEFT: A system of doorways leads the eye through the house.

Connecting spaces

TOP RIGHT: A translucent screen provides definition for different areas of a room without dividing the space structurally.

BOTTOM RIGHT: The removal of part of a dividing wall between a small kitchen and a living area makes the kitchen feel less enclosed.

OPPOSITE: An internal window between two rooms links the different areas and extends the sense of space in both rooms.

BELOW: This first floor bedroom is connected visually and physically to the floor below by an open balcony window.

Typically, our living arrangements are designed as a series of enclosed rooms which use doors to connect and close off one area from another. In certain parts of the home, such as bedrooms and bathrooms, some form of screening is necessary for privacy. However, when we take a closer look at how and why we use space generally, it would seem that for the most part, doors serve no real purpose. Even internal walls themselves can suddenly seem unnecessarily solid and inflexible. Instead of limiting ourselves to the idea of enclosed, individual rooms, we can think about how we might open up the spaces – remove whole walls or sections of wall to connect different areas. In this way our views through the home are extended and the spaces seem to be without end. Such devices can also create a focal point, such as a long succession of rooms ending with doors that lead out onto a garden. Similarly, a setting can be enlivened by a shock of strong tone that sits in the distance of another area. Even when structural alterations are not possible, the simple step of removing a door and streamlining or widening a doorway, can bring a dramatic shift in atmosphere.

Where space needs to be divided or different areas defined, we can think about alternative and flexible options to walls and doors, such as screens that allow light through but mask the view, or sliding doors with glass or opaque panels that can close off an area when required but can also be left open to reveal the whole space. For a truly delicate division, a screen of fabric panels hung from a bamboo rail provides a subtle solution. (See pages 28-29 for details.)

To allow natural light to flow through the home from one room to another, consider introducing internal windows. They are also an excellent device for connecting separate areas and increase the sense of space by extending the horizon. In this picture, an L-shaped figure cut into the wall between a kitchen and living room is all that is needed to link the two rooms.

THIS PAGE: The symmetry of this open plan staircase takes on an almost sculptural quality against the simplicity of the plain white wall.

OPPOSITE: Rooms are connected with sliding screens in this lofty apartment. The blue flooring provides a unifying element that also extends the sense of space.

Every exit is an entry somewhere else.

Tom Stoppard

Walls

Large expanses of plain walls fill many people with unease and an overwhelming desire to cover them with patterns, shelves or a collection of pictures. Empty wall space is often regarded as dull and unimaginative. But in fact, a simple plastered wall can be beautiful in its own right. Effortlessly serene, its uninterrupted continuity is restful. It also serves to emphasize the lines of the architectural style.

Kept truly simple, walls can seem to disappear, making the space between them expand. This illusion works better with pale receding colours than with deep colours. Even exposed brick work can be visually satisfying, with its rhythmic pattern and rough textural interest. Where decoration does remain – such as traditional plaster cornicing in old houses – it becomes an unexpected visual treat against the unadorned walls.

RIGHT: Flat painted walls set against the natural hues of the wooden doors accentuate the structure of a hallway. By keeping the design scheme simple, the clean lines take on an almost sculptural quality, increasing the suggestion of height and space, which is stunningly effective when you consider that this is just a rather ordinary hallway.

LEFT: Natural materials provide the decorative quality for these wall dividers, which give a strong, cohesive and dynamic look to a bathroom.

BOTTOM RIGHT: The elegant form of a wooden hand rail becomes even more striking when set on an empty wall.

BOTTOM LEFT: Harmonizing colours for different sections of wall provide depth and definition in a room and are a useful device for visually altering the dimensions. In an open plan arrangement they can be used to signify separate areas.

Floors

Of all the structural elements, floors – which comprise the largest single surface – have the greatest potential to influence the atmosphere in a room. By using the same treatment throughout, the floor can be used to link separate rooms, suggest continuity between spaces, and bring unity to the overall look. The most successful flooring goes almost unnoticed – it may be textured, made of natural materials, smooth or have a simple pattern – but it should always strive to be an all over effect and never compete with other aspects of the room.

The quiet earthy tones of natural materials, such as wood and stone, and sisal or coir matting, are ideal flooring choices, offering a neutral base to a room. Sanded floorboards are one of the simplest treatments and the easiest to maintain. Polished floorboards bring out the beauty of the grain, whilst 'old' floorboards bring depth and character to a room. Painted boards allow you to introduce colour, as do other less recognized natural products such as linoleum and rubber. Currently enjoying a revival, these last two types of flooring can be bought in a wonderful range of gentle or bright colours. From a practical point of view, these floor coverings tend to be a good choice for kitchens and bathrooms, as they are resilient and easy to keep clean. A calm living space can also find a perfect balance in the creamy smoothness of a painted concrete floor or the warm softness of good quality woollen carpet.

Pattern is important. In a simple setting it should be kept regular and symmetrical – the rhythmic woven texture of natural fibres, the geometric appearance of slate or terracotta tiles – and more complex patterns should be restricted to small areas, such as rugs.

ABOVE: Wooden floorboards running from room to room provide a visual link. Use a rug to add a change in tone and texture.

LEFT: The texture of wickerwork blends beautifully with the woven pattern in a natural floor covering.

FAR LEFT: Woven floor coverings give soft colour to a room without imposing on the simplicity of the scheme.

OPPOSITE: Pale grey floorboards introduce a graphic quality, with the muted colour accentuating the spaces inbetween the boards and creating the appearance of stripes.

27

Linen screen

The translucent quality of the linen panels creates an effect of airiness and light, despite visually separating the two areas of a room.

YOU WILL NEED:

• **150cm/60in wide loose weave linen (or similar furnishing fabric) measuring from the floor to about 30cm/12in below the ceiling, plus 26cm/10³/₄in for turnings**

• **2.3m/92in length of bamboo, 5cm/2in in diameter**

• **2m/80in textured rope**

• **Two large metal hooks**

• **Reel of matching cotton thread and needle**

• **Scrap of fabric or paper**

• **Drill and drill bits**

• **Iron**

NB: if using very lightweight fabric you may need to attach curtain weights (or small coins) at the lower corners of each panel. Cut a small oblong of the screen fabric twice as long as the curtain weight plus 2cm/³/₄in, and 2cm/³/₄in wide. With right sides together, fold the fabric in half lengthways and stitch the side seams together to create a small pouch. Turn right side out. Slip the weight inside and turn in the open edge and hem neatly in place. Sew pockets to each bottom corner of the panel on the wrong side.

1 Working to a maximum width of 150cm/60in, decide on the width of each of the three panels of fabric for the screen by using scrap fabric or paper taped to the bamboo pole and held in position to get an idea of the finished effect. The screen shown here used a central panel of 65cm/26in and two side panels each 42.5cm/17in wide. Neaten the two long sides and one short side by folding the raw edges over twice to the wrong side and machine or hand stitch in place. Press the hems flat.

2 To make a channel at the top of each panel for threading the fabric onto the bamboo pole, tidy the remaining raw edge of each panel by folding over twice to the wrong side. Pin and tack in place. Measure 11cm/4³/₈in down from the hem and fold the fabric over to the wrong side. Pin, tack and then stitch the hem in place by working one row of stitching along the edge of the hem and one row just above it.

3 Drill a hole right through the diameter of the bamboo 10cm/4in in from either end of the pole. Thread the panels of fabric onto the bamboo support, and position in place about 20cm/8in apart.

4 Mark the position for the screen and screw the large hooks into the ceiling corresponding with the position of the holes in the bamboo pole. Using 1m/3ft lengths at each end, thread twine through the holes in the bamboo pole and then tie securely in place to the hooks above, allowing the screen to hang about 30cm/12in from the ceiling so that the panels of fabric sit just clear of the floor. Adjust the position of the panels on the pole if necessary.

When we see only
what lies before us,
our minds have
become clouded by
expectation. But look
out beyond the
horizon, and we find
the freedom of
endless possibility.

windows
extending
horizons

One of the first things we do in the morning is go to a window and look out. Although the view may be familiar, what we see is always different: a bright sunny day and an endless blue sky, the dark drama of rain or even a crisp white blanket of snow. The subtlest changes in light affect the colours we see and the shadows that are cast by trees and buildings. The view can affect us in myriad ways. We may feel invigorated by the seemingly infinite changes of the landscape, or protected from the blustery weather of an autumn day. And as we turn back into our home these feelings remain with us.

Windows break down the boundaries of our home by leading our eyes outwards to the natural world. They increase the perception of space and suggest a greater sense of freedom. Without them, our internal space becomes oppressive and restricting. Think how differently a large open-plan area feels if there are windows at either end offering a glimpse of something more – the space seems infinitely larger and livelier than it would if our eyes suddenly came to a stop at a solid wall.

But we don't have to stand at a window to see what lies beyond. Wherever we are in our home, if a window is within our sight, so too is a view. Without realizing it, the tonal contrasts of a rooftop skyline, the treetops, and the white clouds against a blue sky are all absorbed into the ambience of our home.

It is worthwhile considering how we can make the most of windows. They offer so much as architectural features, in their size, proportions and positioning, and in the quality of light that enters the room. This in turn will affect other design considerations such as the use of colour. If windows are incorporated into the initial decorating plans for a room, they can be exploited to the best of their potential and so improve the atmosphere of the finished area.

Bringing the outside in

Most importantly windows allow us to have a more intimate contact with the outdoors, and where possible, particularly in rooms that sit adjacent to the garden, we should seek to maximize this contact. A room that has the promise of a garden beyond is revitalized by glass doors that lead straight onto a patio or deck. These doors serve to blur the boundaries between interior and exterior by allowing us to see both as we move from one to another. We can further enhance this sensation by choosing similar flooring for both areas – perhaps wooden floorboards inside leading to timber decking outside – and furniture, such as cane or wicker pieces, which further emphasize the appearance of continuity.

LEFT: French doors blur the boundaries of our home – here the exterior and interior appear to be one continuous space.

Letting light in

TOP RIGHT: This once dark and shadowy lobby has been revitalized with a wall of glass bricks.

BOTTOM RIGHT: An open plan setting makes the most of natural daylight flooding in from other areas of the apartment.

BELOW: A former factory has been transformed into a serene, modern home, with a roof that can be opened by remote control.

Most homes suffer from an uneven distribution of light. Some rooms will have a brighter aspect than others; long rooms may be dark at one end, small rooms may not have a window at all; and old houses often have an insufficient number of small windows. But the movement of light within the home does not have to be limited to external windows. There are many creative ways of increasing the amount of light flowing into certain areas.

Windows in internal walls can serve to redistribute light – bringing more light into a dark room – or connect spaces together visually, while keeping the rooms separate. To keep the look simple, choose strong shapes – a medieval slit window

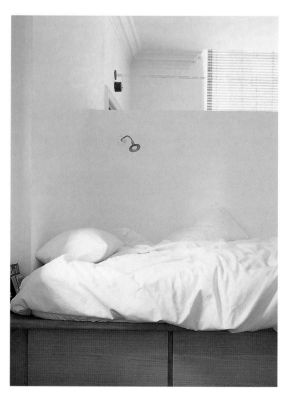

or a large round window – and leave them as open spaces or close them off with a pane of glass. Glass bricks are a wonderful solution for introducing light into darker spaces. A line of glass bricks set into the wall of a gloomy hallway or into a windowless bathroom can instantly enliven the room. Similarly light in a moody landing or stairwell can be improved immeasurably by adding a skylight.

For a truly dramatic effect, you might even consider a whole wall of reinforced glass or glass bricks, so streamlined that no division appears at all. As part of an external wall, this can even make small gardens appear much bigger than they actually are, by connecting them to the larger space indoors. The glass can be clear or coloured. Where privacy is required use opaque glass that has been sandblasted or etched.

If a window looks out onto an uninspiring view there is a wide range of materials available that you can use to decorate the window pane without losing any light coming in. As well as sandblasting and glass etch spray, there is glass paint, or self-adhesive paper, that will colour the light filtering through. Again opt for symmetrical designs to continue the theme of simplicity, or go for bold strong shapes, such as circles, which have decorative clarity. Tracing paper makes an attractive mask, either applied to each pane as a flat haze of opacity, or with patterns cut into the sheets to add interesting shimmers of light.

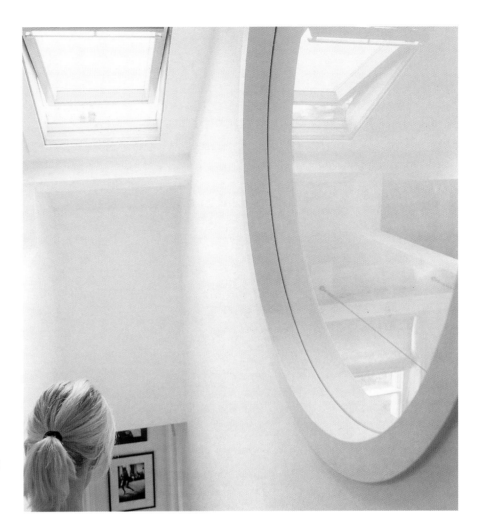

TOP RIGHT: Skylights offer a simple solution to the problem of introducing light into dark hallways or landings.

RIGHT: A line of glass bricks running from wall to wall or ceiling to floor is a stylish way of allowing light to flow from one area to another.

If the doors of perception were cleansed everything would appear to man as it is, infinite.

William Blake

THIS PAGE: A north-facing bedroom is given a more sunny outlook with the installation of internal windows connecting the room to a large open plan living area. Plain roller blinds provide privacy in the evenings.

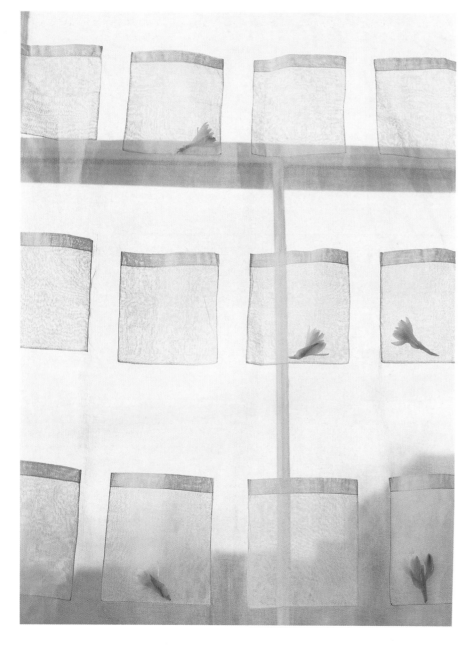

Window dressing

Window treatments can seem an unnecessary addition to the Zen home – why spoil the clean lines of the frame and obscure the view. But in many situations, we need to be able to screen our home off from the outside world, either to provide privacy, insulation, or shade from the sun on a blazing hot day.

The key question is how to retain the uncluttered theme in our surroundings while providing a practical solution for our everyday needs. Traditionally, curtains and window coverings are a decorative treatment in themselves. Unfortunately, they can sometimes be quite imposing and visually busy. The style of window dressing needs to be kept simple and streamlined so that it blends into the room without drawing our attention.

Straight panels of plain fabric that slide along a curtain pole with tabs or ties are one way of overcoming this. When drawn the curtain will hang straight without pleats. By using a curtain pole that is wider than the window, you will be able to pull the curtain right back during the daytime to let the light flood in. Clip or peg semi-sheer fabrics onto curtain wire for a fresh, modern look. The way these fabrics filter and modify the light passing through is wonderfully evocative of the ever-changing quality of natural light outdoors.

By keeping pattern and decoration to a minimum, a simple, informal curtain will not detract from the architectural style of the window. If, however, your taste is for a little ornamentation, look for voile with a delicate pattern incorporated into the fabric that will be enhanced when placed in front of the light. For a straight, flat blind, handmade papers with flecks of plant fibre diffuse the light without impinging on the airy feel of a space. Mirror the theme of strong, clean lines in your curtain style through a line of stitched pockets that hold single dried flowers and leaves, the use of simple decorative stripes (see pages 40-41 for details), or cottons and linens with plain checks.

Fabrics made of natural fibres are the best choice of materials, as their quality lends itself to the most casual style of curtain (see Chapter 4 for a discussion of fabrics). Combined with calm colours, these fabrics will not force a visual break with the surrounding walls.

Roller blinds are another good option, as they can be rolled up during the daytime to maximize the light coming in. Wooden Venetian blinds have a symmetry that is aesthetically pleasing. Left open in a sun-drenched room, they can throw striking patterns of golden stripes across the floors and walls, or closed a little can shield the glare – ideal for home offices. White painted shutters are a good alternative, providing clean straight lines when open and simple shapes when closed across the window at night.

BELOW LEFT: Roller blinds offer the simplest treatment for windows; conservatory blinds that unwind from the bottom upwards can be useful in situations where you want to screen your room from onlookers without blocking out the light.

ABOVE: The hues of wooden slatted blinds add warmth to a room, and their form creates mood and shadow as the light filters through.

OPPOSITE: Add a flamboyant touch to sheer pale fabrics, by adding square pockets to insert natural elements such as flowers and leaves.

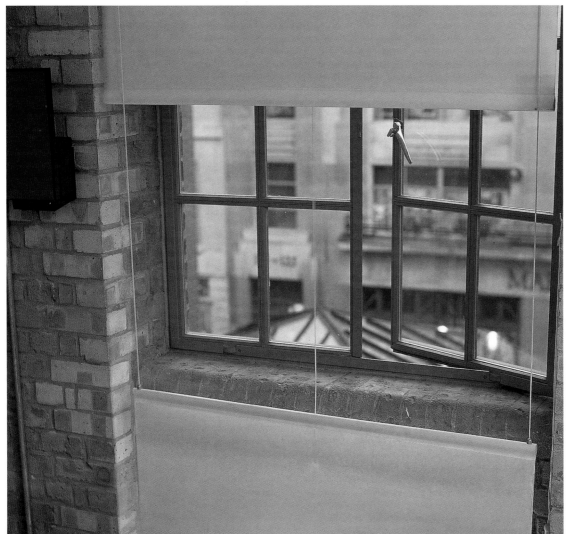

Striped muslin curtain

Create diffused patterns of sunlight with a simple window treatment for a large or small window.

YOU WILL NEED:
• **Length of white cotton muslin measuring the width of the window plus 3cm/1¹/₄in, and the length plus 4.5cm/1³/₄in**
• **1cm/³/₈in wide straight tape in a contrasting colour (enough to run around the outside edge of the finished curtain plus 5cm/2in, plus the width of the finished curtain plus 2cm/³/₄in by the number of horizontal stripes required)**
• **Reel of white cotton sewing thread and needle**
• **Plastic covered spring curtain wire**
• **Two small screw-in hooks**
• **Pencil or dressmaker's chalk**
• **Iron**

1 Neaten the long sides and one short side of the fabric by folding the raw edges over twice to the right side to make a double hem. (Make sure the finished hem is a little narrower than the width of the tape.) Pin, tack and stitch in place. Press the turnings flat.

2 On the right side of the fabric, mark a line 3cm/1¹/₄in down from the remaining short raw edge. (This marks the top of the curtain.) Between this line and the bottom hem of the curtain, divide the length into horizontal stripes, approximately 30cm/12in apart, and mark the positions. Cut strips of tape just less than the width of the curtain and place these centrally across the guide lines. Ensure that the raw edges of the strips lie halfway across the hems down the sides of the curtain. Pin and tack the tape in place and then stitch along the top and bottom edges. Press flat.

3 Cut a length of tape long enough to run around the outer edge of the curtain plus about 5cm/2in. Starting in one corner, pin and tack the tape in place around the edge of the curtain, covering the outer hem and the raw edges of the horizontal stripes, and running across the guideline marked as the top of the curtain.

4 Mitre the tape at the corners as you work your way around the length of fabric. When you reach the corner where you started, turn under the raw edge of tape to create a final mitred corner. Stitch the tape in place by sewing along both edges of the tape as before. Press flat. Fold the remaining fabric at the top of the curtain over to the wrong side using the top stripe of tape as a guide. Turn under 1cm/³/₈in to neaten and hem stitch along the edge catching in the back of the curtain. Thread the curtain wire through this channel and fix the curtain in the window using the two small hooks.

colour
in touch with the senses

Only in the palest of
settings can we experience
the true glory of colour.

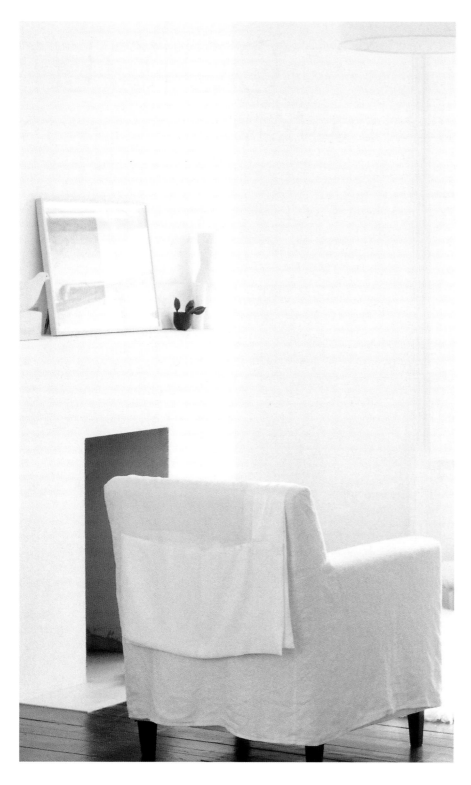

Colour is one of the most potent elements found in nature. We see it everywhere, and are touched by the sensation of it, responding intuitively to it without thought: the luscious shade of a fabric that makes us want to reach out and touch, the edible redness of a bowl of fresh strawberries that tantalizes our tastbuds, and the muted hues of a favourite landscape that can remind us of childhood memories. We don't just see colour, we experience it.

If colour is a vital part of our lives, then it is an equally important part of our home. Without colour our senses are not fully alive. But what are we hoping for when we use colour in the home? Do we see and experience colour more acutely as a bold and daring blaze of bright yellow painted walls or do we find it in the intensity of a single yellow flower? Can the subtle shift in tone of cream and white be just as visually powerful as a sensational pattern or striking contrast? Real use of colour is all about realizing its full potential, both as something to be seen and as something to be experienced. And often it is in its simplest

LEFT: The quality of different materials and surfaces brings tonal variation in this room of pure white.

even the soap we have in our bathroom. All these ingredients work together to make up the colour schemes we bathe our home in.

The palette for the Zen home takes inspiration from the colours found on earth, from the transient blues of seasonal skies, lakes and oceans, to the greens of moss, duck eggs and mountain pines, and the browns of soil and tree bark. Neutrals are a powerful influence, from the cereal shades of crops and honey hues of bamboo and rattan to the greys of pebbles and stones and the whites of snow, scudding clouds and the crests of a fast-running woodland stream. Into this neutral backdrop, the purity of a deep colour used in isolation intensifies.

These colours find their best expression in natural dyes, which give a quiet beauty to fabrics used for soft furnishings, and as the colours fade with age, the effect only adds to the inherent beauty of the fabric. Paint manufacturers produce an incredible wealth of shades to simulate the colours of nature, but in the truest sense of Zen, we should seek our chosen colours among the available range of organic paints (see Chapter 10).

form, uncluttered by other things, that we see it with most clarity.

But colour is not just a thing of beauty, it is also a dynamic tool that can be used to change the sense of space in a room, emphasizing detail and providing cohesion and continuity of style. It can imbue a room with atmosphere, create a sense of calm – even affect our moods.

Most importantly, colour in the home is about balance and proportion – not only in relation to the structure of the home and the atmosphere we are trying to create, but also between the different colours we use within it, whether similar shades or startling opposites. Set vibrant pink beside purple, for example, and they reduce each other to a muddy clash of tones, but set them in equal proportions against white, and they come alive with energy and vitality.

And colour, of course, doesn't just come come in paint pots. We find it amongst all the things we choose to surround ourselves with, from fabrics and flooring to the natural tones of wood, saucepans, storage jars, plants and flowers,

Purity

White is by far the purest of colours to use in the home. It manages to bring freshness and light to our surroundings, working well with almost any other colour we may wish to introduce. It has an amazing ability to unify the setting, extending the feeling of space and providing a common ground for the most disparate of elements.

It works beautifully in any home. In a modern minimalist apartment, it is a perfect backdrop for collectibles and modern furniture. At the other extreme, a busy traditional interior can be calmed and simplified with the introduction of a shade of white.

Using white doesn't mean that a home has to become a museum, or a place that cannot accommodate children. Indeed, if we are to feel relaxed at home we need to be able to live without constant worries and fears for our surroundings. Buy sofas and chairs that have removable covers, or make loose covers from quality cotton, all of which are machine washable, and apply paints on walls that can be wiped down. White, after all is timeless; as a wall colour it provides a versatile setting into which the smallest changes or additions of colour can reap dramatic results. As a basic investment, it is likely to endure over the years more than any other colour.

Within the single colour there is a wealth of nuances of shade – the hard blue edge of brilliant white, the warmer gentleness of standard white, and the many hints including chalk white, ecru, eggshell and bone, through to creams and the palest of beige. The quality of white is also changed by the material of which it is a part – the smooth sheen of white china, the textural crispness of linen, the translucence of muslin or the 'patina' of an old whitewashed wall. Using these different materials in a setting can create a look that has softness as well as interest.

Combining the different shades allows you to create delicate changes of mood and depth. Build up the layers by choosing variations of shade for walls, woodwork, architraves and textiles.

RIGHT: In an all-white setting, the gentle changes of tone in the materials and paints become apparent, creating definition and interest.

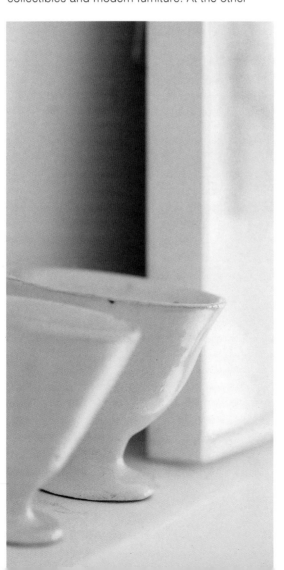

Harmony

A white setting can often provide the perfect background for gentle touches of earthy colour. Used sparingly, neutrals can be utilized to good effect, helping to highlight a particular architectural feature, exaggerate the symmetry of a room or add interest. A section of wall jutting into a white surrounding, for example, or the recesses either side of a fireplace, become more striking when painted in a different shade to the rest of the room, and can even appear to add depth by accentuating the structure. Plain cupboard doors, inset into a wall and painted in a complementary shade to the wall colour, can be a simple way of breaking up the expanse of white without diffusing the simplicity of the architecture. Indeed, a block of soft colour heightens the impact of clean, straight lines.

Create harmony as well through the combination of colours. Balance two colours of a similar intensity, or source colours from the same tonal band to decorate a room so that there is uniformity even in variety. Similarly, use the same tonal band from one room to another to bring a cohesive force to the overall scheme.

Think about how other items might be used in juxtaposition to harmonize the elements of a space: for instance the slate grey of a pile of stones on a white painted floor; a scattering of aubergine or muted brown cushions on a mauve sofa; the warm wheaten yellow of a willow chair in a cool white setting; even a row of glass storage jars filled with pasta and rice. These are all simple ways to harmonize different colours in a single space.

LEFT: Natural colours and textures provide warmth in a cool white setting.

BELOW: A black and white scheme for the bed works perfectly in this pared-back setting, because neither colour dominates.

What is the colour
of the wind?

Zen Koan

THIS PAGE: A gradation of tones through blue and lilac bring a serene harmony of colour.

TOP: A deep pink is used to accentuate the side of the staircase and the struts of the stairwell in an otherwise white apartment.

LEFT: The clean shape of an empty fireplace is accentuated with a vivid shock of blue.

Accent

In the simplest of settings, a single note of brazen colour shines out, because we see it in isolation rather than as part of a tapestry of colours. Restrained use of a strong colour will add extra dimension to a room.

The placement of a colour accent, however, requires careful consideration. Resist the urge to rush in with your favourite bright colour: get to know your space and always keep the look simple and uncluttered. For maximum effect, keep the use of accents to a minimum, and keep to just one colour.

Rather than using striking colour for obvious areas, such as below a dado rail or in a recess, or for the more common paint effects such as a series of vertical or horizontal stripes around a room which detract from the architectural style rather than accentuate it, use a confident burst of colour to emphasize a staircase or highlight the form and structure of a mezzanine floor. Look for bold shades of wall paint, from deep red to fuchsia, sunflower yellow to citrus green, to emphasize a particular feature, such as a fireplace, or break with the clean lines of the architectural style altogether with an asymmetrical jolt of colour to release and refresh the spirit. A bold vertical stripe of colour running from floor to ceiling increases the sense of height in a room, as well as providing a refreshing burst of colour. It can also function to demarcate different living areas. (See pages 52-53 for details.)

It is also in the details that we find potent bursts of colour: deep-red or rust orange cushions add an exotic flavour to a neutral coloured bedroom; vivid blue or yellow around doorways or window frames lift a plain, white hallway; and citrus coloured bowls, frosted glass vases of single long-stemmed orchids or lilies in the kitchen create a warm, summery feel.

ABOVE: Fresh flowers are a wonderful source of bright colours and offer a simple way to add accent to a simple colour scheme.

LEFT: A white bathroom is given a buzz with accessories in lime green.

Textured stripe

A vertical stripe of mottled colour gives striking definition to pale surroundings.

YOU WILL NEED:
- **Tester pot of ivory or off white matt emulsion**
- **Tester pot of bright blue matt emulsion**
- **Lint free cloth**
- **Wide masking tape**
- **Plumb line or spirit level**
- **Lining paper or spare paper for testing**
- **Medium sized paintbrush**
- **Sheets of old newspaper**
- **Damp cloth**
- **Soft pencil and eraser**

NB: Before starting to paint the actual stripe onto a wall, practise the paint effect on some lining paper until you achieve a result you are happy with. Depending on the height of the wall, you may also want to adjust the width of the stripes.

1 To set the position for the blue stripe, use a plumb line or spirit level, to mark two vertical lines on the wall, 3.5cm/1³/₄in apart, from the lower edge of the wall to the ceiling. Run masking tape down the outer edge of each line to create an outline for the stripe. Run masking tape along the ceiling and on the woodwork or floor at the base of the wall to protect these areas from paint. Remove some of the stickiness of the tape by pressing it onto another surface before applying it to the wall. (This ensures you won't pull any paint off the wall when you peel the masking tape away).

2 Dampen your paintbrush slightly and charge with blue paint. Remove any excess paint by dabbing the brush onto a piece of newspaper. (Your brush should be quite dry so that when you draw it along the wall it leaves a mottled texture). Starting from the top, use light, downward strokes to cover the exposed area with paint. You may need to recharge your brush two or three times to complete the stripe. Work quickly and cover the whole area before the paint dries.

3 Immediately after applying the paint, wipe the stripe with a damp cloth using downward strokes. This smoothes out the texture of the paint and removes some areas of colour to create a subtle, patchy finish. Work the entire length of the stripe, reworking areas lightly to achieve the finished effect. Allow the paint to dry for a few hours. Clean the paintbrush thoroughly.

4 Remove the left-hand strip of masking tape. Measuring from the left-hand edge of the remaining strip, mark one vertical line 2cm/³/₄in away and another 22cm/8⁵/₈in away. Mask the outside area of these markers as before to create a second stripe slightly overlapping the blue one. Apply ivory paint in the same way as before. Remove all the masking tape and allow the paint to dry.

texture and materials

nature as inspiration

We are but as a pebble or a piece of wood –
of nature and part of nature.

The modern world takes us further and further away from our place in nature. New technology, the towering forms of cities and towns, the noise and pollution of traffic are the negative aspects that over-whelm us and dampen our spirits. By contrast, contact with nature seems to replenish the soul – whether it is an escape to the green, open countryside or a walk along the beach, a trip to the park, or just time spent in the garden. From these trips we invariably bring back a leaf or a pebble and place it on a shelf or mantlepiece to remind our-selves of the experience.

Nature is a great leveller. Its sheer scale is breathtaking. In the presence of the awe-inspiring and the minutiae, other things rapidly become less significant – and suddenly it seems easier to decide what is important in life.

Nature is also about simple pleasures. The joy of witnessing the cycle of changes throughout the year – the excitement at seeing the first shoots of spring appear, watching them grow and blossom and then fade away to begin all over again. This

sense of continuity is written down in the patterns of nature – the rings on the bark of a tree and the ancient seams in a rock – and in seeing them, we are reminded that we are also part of the natural world and this connection provides us with a sense of belonging and a place in time. When we bring natural elements into our home, we bring all these qualities too.

We can look to the natural world to provide inspiration in our decorating style, through furni-ture, flooring, the way we decorate our walls and adorn our windows, and in the details and acces-sories that allow us to make creative use of found objects. But using natural materials to enrich our homes should not at the same time impoverish the environment. We must be careful not to squander what has taken years to grow. Where possible look for opportunities to re-cycle. For example, it is now quite easy to source old wooden floorboards and furniture from salvaging companies. And perhaps, instead of buying new, scour junk shops and market stalls for pieces to use or transform.

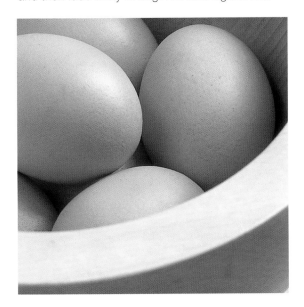

OPPOSITE: The patterns and textures of nature embody a sense of time and continuity. We can draw inspiration from this spiritually, and as a source for ideas in our home.

Pattern and texture

Myriad patterns present in nature are ornament enough in themselves. Sit back, look and enjoy – and then touch. For you cannot help but want to feel the surface of a gnarled piece of driftwood, the woven structure of a cane chair or the sleek surface of smooth granite. In this way, our home becomes more than just a setting to look at, it becomes tactile as well.

If you want a restful interior, you can create interest through the innate irregular patterns and textures of natural materials, that provide a contrast to the more rigid lines and geometric patterns of the architectural style. Quiet patterns allow you to use natural materials as a backdrop, such as the veins in a marble sink and the grain in wooden floorboards; interesting shapes allow you to use them as details and finishing touches, such as a conch on a mantlepiece. Introduce texture through perennial grasses such as reeds and bamboo woven into wall hangings, screens and blinds, and pieces of driftwood or bark threaded onto lengths of leather to make a bathmat. Think too about the sensation of a material – the coldness of a stone floor stimulates the feet, while the warmth of wood is more soothing.

We can also use the patterns and textures in nature to inspire our own creativity in the home – roughened surfaces, mottled effects, chalky substances – all of these can be interpreted into decorative effects. A layer of white or off-white colour wash applied to raw plaster (which should then be sealed with varnish), takes on a subtle patchy appearance as the plaster absorbs the colour in different intensities. Used on a single

wall or partition, it helps break up the flat areas of colour. Or try a white plaster finish which has an inherent mottled effect and simply seal with varnish. For a more dramatic look, use marmorino, a plaster finish mixed with marble dust. It adds a stone-like quality to a wall and can be highly polished to add lustre. Similarly a white painted wall, colour-washed with ecru, takes on a hint of texture that is barely noticeable.

BELOW: A set of utilitarian wooden spoons can be used to create a collection of rich colour and interesting shape.

RIGHT: A worn and battered piece of driftwood has a unique history, the passing of time woven into its grain and the personal memory of the moment when it was found.

OPPOSITE: A sheet of slate makes a glorious chiselled surface for a table.

To see a World in a grain of sand,
And a Heaven in a wild flower,
Hold infinity in the palm of your hand,
And eternity in an hour.

William Blake

Textiles

Fabrics provide a whole wealth of textures, and their subtlety can be used effectively in the simplicity of the Zen home. In a setting that is cool, pared-back, with a concentration on clean lines and shapes, textiles used for soft furnishings inject a vital dimension of warmth and comfort – the feel of crisp cotton sheets against the skin; the luxuriance of sinking into velvet cushions; the soothing quality of diffused sunlight through an organza curtain.

The natural fibres of cotton, linen and wool are ideal for the home, as they allow the skin to breathe, unlike synthetic materials, such as nylon, which do not. More importantly, these fabrics come from renewable resources.

Cotton is probably the most versatile of the natural fabrics, used on all types of soft furnishings. Made from the seed fibre of the cotton plant, the yarn is woven into a tough fabric that is extremely receptive to dyes. The term covers a whole range of materials from cotton lawn whose light freshness is ideal for sheets and pillow cases, through to softer calico for cushions and blinds and voile for a simple sheath at the window.

Linen comes from another annual plant. The long fibres of flax are combed and spun into yarn, which is used to make linen of various qualities from coarse slub to fine matt. The finished fabric is immensely strong and hardwearing and as it ages its appearance will only improve. Linens look their best in natural, pale, or earthy colours, such as oatmeal. Hung unlined against a window, the woven pattern, with its irregularities, will come to

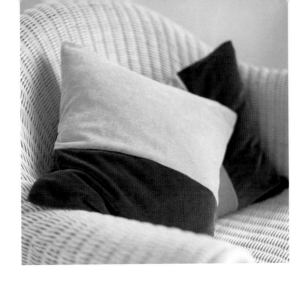

the fore producing a gentle pattern. Use it lined for a more dramatic, heavier look. If you feel a little more decorative detail is necessary, linen and cotton lend themselves well to drawn-thread work and simple embroidery that do not detract from the essential character of the weave.

While cotton and linen are cool to the touch, wool is warm and springy. Fleece is prepared into wool fibres that can be woven or knitted to produce a range of textures. Choose from the regular weaving of a blanket or throw to the curly detail of wool bouclé on cushions.

Silk is the most luxurious of the natural fabrics. Made from the the tough filaments of silkworm cocoons, it comes in a variety of weights and textures. Silk has a special radiance dyed in the vivid colours of the orient. Use it sparingly in the Zen home for colour and textural accents. Hang chiffon at the window and use the nubbly surface of raw silk for a couple of elegant cushions.

Hessian is the heaviest of the fabrics, made from the fibres of the jute plant, or a mixture of jute and hemp. Used in the past for wall coverings, it is a suitable material for curtains when you want to achieve a heavier, rugged look.

LEFT: Lush velvet cushions with an asymmetrical design create a point of interest against the woven symmetry of the wicker chair. (See pages 64-65 for details.)

OPPOSITE: Crisp white bed linen makes a stunning contrast to the honey tones of the wooden frame.

BELOW: The inherent weave in fabric is a decorative treat in itself; use a blend of different fabrics together to create softness and interest.

Velvet cushion covers

Add a touch of warmth and pattern to surroundings with sumptuous textures and rich natural hues.

YOU WILL NEED:

• **Square cushion pad measuring 40cm/16in**
• **Brown cotton velvet measuring 52 x 42cm/21 x 17in**
• **Cream cotton velvet measuring 52 x 42cm/21 x 17in**
• **Reel of matching cotton thread and needle**
• **Sewing machine**
• **Measuring tape**
• **Iron**

1 Place the two pieces of velvet right sides together and sew a 1cm/³/₈in seam along one short side. Press the seam open.

2 You will now have one long strip of fabric. Neaten each end by folding 2cm/³/₄in under to the reverse side and fix in place with herringbone stitch. Press flat.

3 Lay the fabric on a clean flat surface with right side uppermost. From the neatened edge of the brown cotton, measure one third the length of your cushion pad, fold over and pin (wrong side now uppermost); from the neatened edge of the cream cotton measure two thirds the length of your cushion, fold over and pin in the same way (neatened edge will overlap the brown velvet by 9cm/3⁵/₈in).

4 Pin, tack and machine sew along the top and bottom edges of the cushion cover across the overlap of the two pieces of material with a 1cm/³/₈in seam allowance. Trim the seam turnings, press, and turn the cushion cover right side out. The overlapping neatened edges form the opening through which to insert the cushion pad.

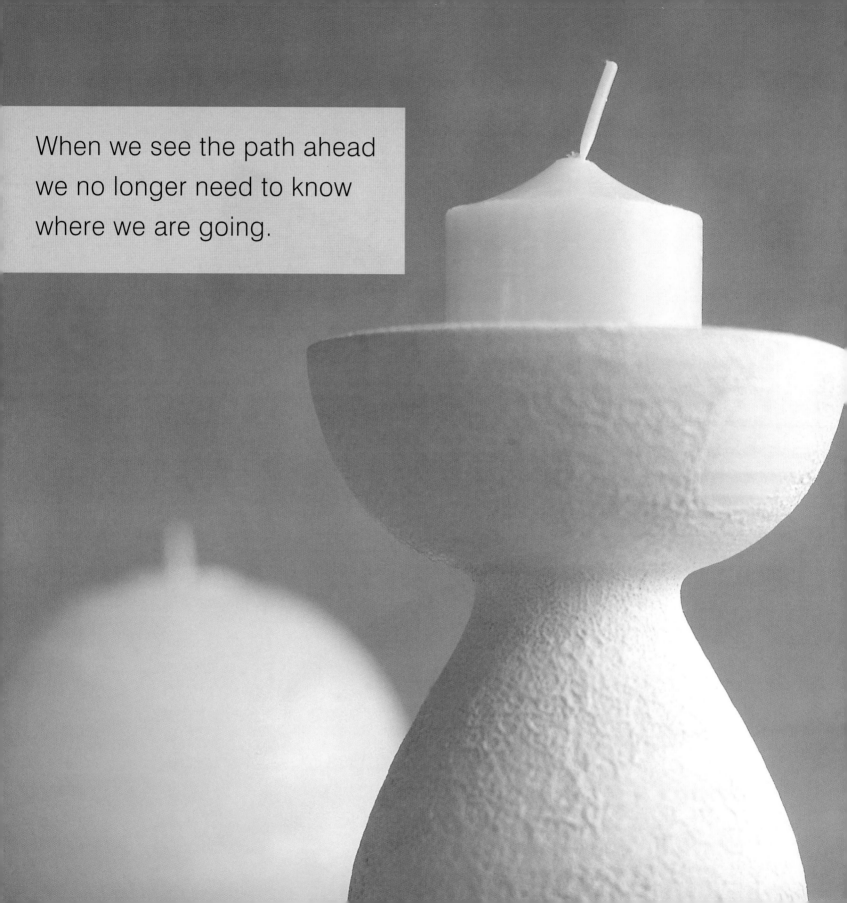

When we see the path ahead
we no longer need to know
where we are going.

lighting

tranquility and atmosphere

Lighting is something we rarely stop and think about and yet, it affects us just as much as colour and space. Light plays a major role in creating ambience in a room. We are drawn to places where the light is in harmony with our mood, from the revitalizing feel of a sunlit day to the tranquility of a room lit solely by candle-light. If the Zen home is a place where we can unwind and open our minds, then the impact of light on our surroundings is of prime importance. But the Zen home is also a place where many activities occur, and we need to make sure that we have sufficient light in order to complete them.

LEFT: Lighting can provide decorative elements to the home as well as enhancing mood and ambience.

BELOW: Simple forms meld with the surrounding design and become an elegant visual aspect as well as a practical light source.

While we may spend hours choosing furniture or deciding on the colour scheme for our home, we often give very little thought to lighting, either natural or artificial. We take the pervading mood for granted, as though it is something that is set and without possibilities for improvement.

Lighting is often chosen as an afterthought when everything else is completed or planned. But in fact, the way in which we exploit the natural day-light, and add further shape to our surroundings with artificial illumination, can have a huge impact on a room.

We need to consider lighting at the earliest stages of decoration, planning how to best incorporate the natural source and then how that can be backed up with additional lighting. Without giving attention to lighting we miss an opportunity to make the most of a space or room, changing its rhythms whenever we want to create the appropriate atmosphere for socializing, working, reading, preparing food or watching television at the end of a long day.

The light of life

RIGHT: The sun is our greatest source of vitality.

OPPOSITE: Large windows make the most of natural sunlight and uplift the colour scheme of any room.

BELOW: Shafts of sunlight throw shadows across the wall.

Sunlight is the force of life, and just like the plants that open to its warmth, so we too become more cheerful and positive when it is shining. Over the millennia, we have adapted to the seasonal cycles, and our bodies' circadian rhythms and biological clocks are timed to perfection to follow the movement from dark to light, winter through to summer. We have also become aware of how much we are subtley affected by light – some people are so affected by sunlight, or the lack of it, that they suffer from a condition called SAD (Seasonal Affective Disorder) which is characterized by depression, fatigue, tiredness, weight gain, and a craving for carbohydrates in the dark winter months. With this in mind, it makes sense to use the natural light entering our homes efficiently.

To harness it, we must first understand it – that means getting to know a room, spending time in the space at different times of the day to see when the light is at its best, how the light flows and the colours and patterns it creates. The natural light that enters a room during the day is its focus and soul, the source from which everything else comes to life. Although the amount of natural light entering the home is set by the windows, we can make efforts to highlight, shape and utilize it to the best advantage (see Chapter 2).

If the home is newly built or you have recently moved in, consider this light when deciding how to allocate each room – a room that has the best light in the afternoon and early evening might be better used as a living room; whereas, a room that receives light in the morning is more suited to a bedroom or kitchen situation; and a room that has

light all day long would be good for a home office for those who work permanently from home. The changing nature of light should be taken into consideration when thinking about structural alterations. If for example, you are removing walls or doorways to create an open plan living space, arrange the layout so that the light can shine through. A corner or area where there is always good light, for example, can be a prime position for a desk or reading area. A room that receives very strong sunlight for prolonged periods can sometimes have a negative impact, forcing us to shield our eyes and making us feel hot and flustered. In this instance, think about ways to control the amount of light rather than trying to maximize its potential.

The quality of light can also influence decorative decisions. If the light is bright and golden then additional colour to a pale scheme might seem unnecessary; in a place where it is cool, use of warmer colours might be a better option to add a sense of depth and spirit to an area. And in a place where glorious splashes of light are formed across the walls and floors, other elements may be kept to a minimum and lines and details kept simple to allow the light patterns to become the main focus.

Light as practical

Although natural sunlight is the preferred choice for illuminating the home, artificial lighting is often the only option we have, especially in colder climates or during the winter months. But artificial lighting can still have a remarkable effect in the Zen home when used correctly. And indeed, if we are to find more pleasure in everyday tasks, then good lighting, which can also make a job easier, is just as important as aesthetic considerations. Practical lighting needs to be well thought through but it also needs to be discreetly set so as not to confuse or clutter the streamlined view. Practical lighting comes in the form of ambient and task lighting.

The former of these creates the general ambience of a room. It should be flexible so that it can be altered to suit lighting needs throughout the day, but so well designed that we barely notice it. In large areas it becomes the understudy for natural daylight, in smaller, more enclosed situations, it illuminates our way without fuss. Task lighting directs light into a particular discreet area, such as over a desk, or beside a bed for reading.

RIGHT: Recessed lighting in the ceiling of this kitchen illustrate well thought out illumination for practical tasks without detracting from the style and simplicity of the room.

In most rooms try using a variety of light sources – downlights, spotlights, tungsten-halogen uplighters, and desk lights – to achieve a flexible lighting scheme that covers all the activities that will go on in that room. Try to avoid fluorescent lights as they can make you tired and irritable – if you have to use them at all, try and replace the tube for a natural-daylight one.

Assess how each room is used, and where different tasks are performed. In a kitchen, a lighting system in the ceiling with the option to 'direct' the light to different areas, works well – if attached to a dimmer switch a softer mood can be created in the evening, especially useful where there is an dining area within the same room. If wall cupboards are set over work surfaces, lighting can be tucked underneath to throw light down into the shadowy area below and directly onto the place where food is being prepared. A hallway requires a continuous distribution of light flowing through the space – again, recessed ceiling lights can be discreet and effective, but make sure there are enough placed at regular intervals to create one whole sense of light rather than a series of pools. Although a living area requires mood and coziness at night, a backdrop of uniform lighting is equally important for darker days and times when we want good, clean illumination. Again, we want to create a continuous spread of light that lifts the room rather than filling it with shadows. Consider setting these lights in groups connected to a series of switches – in this way we have the option for lowering the level of light or just illuminating one selected area, and this can be useful for creating a more relaxed atmosphere in the evening.

The style of light is an important consideration. Recessed lights that can be fitted flush with the

LEFT: Downlighters provide a directional light for bedtime reading.

ceiling are one of the most low-key options. The angle of light can be directed, just as with conventional spots, but the appearance is more sleek and less imposing than fittings which hang from the ceiling. Fine halogen lights set on a taut wire running across a room, also have a simple appearance – the straight lines of the cable serve to reflect the lines of the architectural structure. In a functional room, such as a kitchen, the simple outline of spotlights can work well as a foil to the utilitarian aspect of the fittings – opt for clean, simple shapes in white or chrome rather than convoluted designs in bright colours. Anglepoise lamps, which are excellent for providing directed light over a desk area, have undergone something of a style transformation and can be a sleek addition to a room while still being practical. Choose slim, streamlined looks that retain a sense of simplicity.

The moment we are enlightened within, We go beyond the voidness of a world confronting us.

Zen Haiku

RIGHT AND BELOW: Look for striking clear shapes for lamps that can become a decorative focus in a room as well as supplying a diffused source of light.

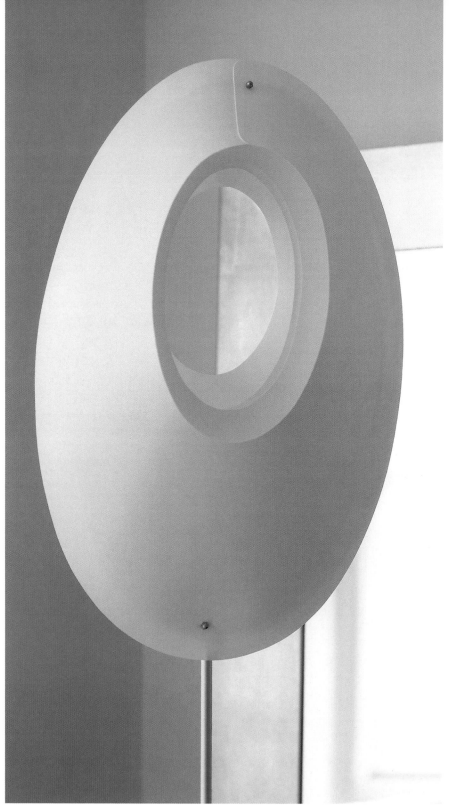

Light as design

Decorative lighting is most often utilized during the evenings or for entertaining when a relaxed and tranquil setting is preferred.

The choice will be dictated by the space and the mood desired for that area. Over a dining table, a single pendant light that can be raised or lowered focuses an area and draws everyone into the conversation. Table lamps are more suitable for living rooms, generating a sensual overall glow and a relaxed feel. Choose several with complementary shapes and designs and dot them around the room. Elsewhere architectural features or pictures can be highlighted with wall lights, and furniture can be lit from below with lights set into the floor to create dramatic shadows. And don't forget candles. Their flickering dancing light is enjoyable to watch and helps to create a mellow atmosphere in which to unwind.

As well as thinking about the quality of light created, it is also important to consider how the fitting itself will sit in the setting. Consider the form of the light and the shape of the shade. Look for arresting shapes, such as the scultural form of a tall table or floor lamp that will throw a crisp silhouette against the backdrop of a wall. (See pages 76-77 for details.) A string of small square shades across a room can create a thread of delicate light which forms its own patterns, and can be hung or coiled to suit your purpose.

It is worth bearing in mind that decorative lighting has to balance decorative elements with function and that shades have to look as good during the day when the light is not illuminated as they do when turned on at night. Think about buying or making your own shade from the range of exquisite papers that are available, such as parchment, or Japanese shoji paper. These can easily be decorated with simple stencils, cut paper work or a raffia or wool edging.

To create a harmonious room setting it is best to think about decorative lighting in conjunction with practical lighting. In this way you can balance the different sources – the style of the light fittings and lamps, and their positions. A few lower wattage lights, spread around an area, are gentler on the eye – and the soul – than one harsh light. You may need to experiment with the wattage and type of bulb in your lighting scheme to achieve the desired effect.

Similar considerations should be made for outdoors. Think how the view out into a garden can be enjoyed after dark by the careful placement of outdoor lights. Instead of looking out into a black hole, a subtle glow leads the eye onwards into the space, so that even in the confines of darkness our horizons seem more open.

LEFT: The glow of candlelight brings a sense of peace and calm to any room.

Table lamp

The fine pattern of ribbed card formed into a curved silhouette creates a striking light source for any room

YOU WILL NEED:
- **A1 sheet of ribbed white card (or similar stiff card)**
- **Piece of card for template**
- **White electrical tape**
- **Slim lamp stand**
- **Large knitting needle**
- **Scissors or Stanley knife**
- **Tracing paper**
- **Ruler**
- **Pencil**

1 Cut a 2cm/³/₄in strip along the length of the card (this will form the cuff at the base of the lamp). Enlarge the template to 59cm/23in tall (you will need to photocopy the template in two halves). Trace this onto the card and cut out the shape with a pair of sharp scissors.

2 Starting about 1cm/³/₈in from the right hand edge of your piece of ribbed card, make three outlines of the template, each set about 18cm/7¹/₈in apart at the base. Position the template a fourth time, as before, but only draw around the right hand side. Cut out the card around the outlines at either end. Gently score the remaining outlines drawn on the card with a pair of scissors or a Stanley knife, taking care not to cut right through the card. Bend the card along these scored lines so that you are able to form the card into a cylinder.

3 Cut about 15 short strips of electrical tape and fix them to a firm surface so that they are easy to pick up. Using the knitting needle, gently work a small hole about 3cm/1¹/₄in in from one of the shaped edges of the card and about 2cm/³/₄in up from the base (this hole will be for the electrical cable of the lamp stand). Bend the card round so that the shaped edges meet; place the pre-cut pieces of tape across the seam on the inside, working the entire length of the join to keep the edges in place.

4 Fold the 2cm/³/₄in strip of card in half lengthways, wrong sides together. Wrap the cuff around the base of the lamp, snipping one half of the cuff to the fold line at each corner. Trim off any excess. Cut about 15 short strips of electrical tape as before. Placing the uncut section of cuff around the outside of the lamp so that the cut section sits underneath to form a small flat stand, line up the snipped sections with the corners of the base. Use the strips of tape positioned on the inside of the base to secure the cuff in place, overlapping the snipped sections at corners so that the cuff sits flat. Position the lamp stand inside lamp and thread the cord out through hole at the back. Attach the plug.

If we define rather than divide, our homes become a series of pathways leading us to new places of discovery.

furniture
shaping the space

No matter how good our surrounding space feels, the true measure of success still comes down to the way in which we use it and are able to live in it. If we are to find a sense of calm and balance in the Zen home, we must first feel comfortable as well as be able to carry out daily tasks efficiently and with enjoyment. Our home should fit us like a glove, existing snugly around us, not constricting us in any way. This involves introducing furniture that provides a balance between decoration and simplicity, function and aesthetics, and the placement of items that allow freedom of movement around the home while creating spaces for activities such as socializing or working.

ABOVE AND BELOW: Wooden and wicker furniture provides an opportunity to add texture to our home and introduce natural elements.

While we make efforts to heighten the sense of space and light in our homes, it is the furniture that determines how well the space actually functions. For this reason, our choice of furniture must always be a personal one, directed by an acute understanding of what we want from our home together with how we like to organize the rooms within it; for instance do we want a combined kitchen, dining and living room, using the furniture itself to define these areas. On a fundamental level there is nothing worse than a kitchen that isn't planned with the way we like to cook in mind – cooking utensils on the other side of the room to the oven, or wall cupboards too high up to access easily. Instead of getting pleasure from preparing food we find ourselves constantly irritated and frustrated. Similarly a wonderful wooden chair might look sublime, but if it is impossible to sit on for any length of time, it will stand unused and become cold and hard to look at. And there is little point contemplating the idea of high-backed armchairs in your living room, if what you really love is a soft, enveloping sofa to sink into. Our goal might be simplicity and a streamlined look, but we cannot achieve this if our surroundings fail to nourish our soul.

OPPOSITE: A combination of wood and metal is used throughout this kitchen from the units to the built-in table and the stools to emphasize a cohesive look.

Furniture decides the dynamics of a room. Whether a run of kitchen units, a bed, or chairs around a table, the shapes and arrangement of furniture breaks up the space, creating new areas within it while retaining the sense of one open area. We can create different 'rooms' within a single space by drawing on the furniture (rather than the structure) to define the different activities such as sitting, dining or working. For example, we achieve the sense of coziness and enclosure that a traditional living room gives us by gathering a sofa and armchairs together in a group – when

we sit there we have a sense of being in a 'room' while still remaining part of a larger space. The general result is a series of connected 'rooms', separate but not divided. These pockets of space alter our view of a room, providing different angles from which to see our surroundings and so enriching our experience of the objects and elements within it.

In addition to providing us with the kind of contentment and organization that we desire, furniture must also find a level of harmony with the back-

The real voyage of discovery consists not in seeking new landscapes, but in having new eyes.

Marcel Proust

drop of the room as well as a sense of balance between the various pieces themselves. Just as with other elements in a home, we need to consider how to incorporate colour, texture, form and decoration without detracting from the general openness of an area. Rather than thinking of furniture as a separate component, we should think of it as a device by which we extend the style and simplicity of our surroundings.

In keeping with the pared-down look of the Zen home, try to opt for less rather than more. Choose pieces for their purity of design, making sure that form reflects the function – whether for practical or relaxation purposes. If you find that there are pieces that you can't use or don't want, take them to your local charity shop.

RIGHT: In an open plan arrangement, a table and chairs grouped at one end of the room creates a natural dining area.

BELOW: Each piece of furniture can be enjoyed in isolation for the qualities it brings to a room. Here a leather chair blends quietly with the other simple decorative aspects of the room.

Relaxation

Comfort and relaxation are vital components of Zen style. If we cannot fully relax, then we cannot fully calm our minds. Furniture should be simple and functional and combine good support with comfort. Look for items that are well designed and you will find that elegant and pleasing form usually follows.

When we relax, we invariably want to lounge or lie down. The two items of furniture we turn to on these occasions are the sofa and the bed. Look for streamlined, organic shapes for your sofa in which to sink and feel cocooned. While the sofa is a one-stop comfort zone where we can entertain or curl up when we are not at work, it is still our bed which is the prime place of relaxation, a place where we spend one third of our lives. We derive safety from the combination of the solid bed frame softened by the mattress, the inviting coolness of fresh bed linen and the all-enveloping warmth of a duvet or blanket. To truly relax, we need to be free of irritation, to simply sit or lie back and allow our senses to roam. As a result, these items need to be able to mix good support with softness. Mattresses that are not well sprung do not offer a good night's rest. Old sofas that have broken or damaged springs do not provide the requisite comfort to allow us to switch off. Choose strong sturdy frames, good upholstery (that you may have to pay that little bit extra for) and the healthy qualities of natural fibres in your choice of mattress, duvet, pillows and sofa cushions.

The warm, rich, natural colour of bamboo and rattan bring an air of easy-living into the home. Their association with life outdoors on patios and verandahs introduces a breezy quality to your interior style. Whole or split canes are used extensively in furnituremaking, woven or plaited into sturdy chairs, chaise longues, sofa bases and table tops. The designs that are produced provide solid support but enough give to enable you to relax enjoying the experiential quality.

A relaxed interior can also be found in the choice of furniture items that are free of excess ornamentation, allowing the eye to rest on the graceful forms and materials of which they are made. This is especially true of wooden furniture. One of the most constant elements of home furnishing styles, wood brings a sense of the past into the home. It lasts for centuries and its beauty endures. Look out especially for pieces made from reclaimed wood – many cabinetmakers and craftspeople will select this, as it is of superior quality to modern-day cuts. This furniture also tends to be well made using traditional techniques by people with a sensitivity to the material they are using and its value. If you do buy new, try to source furniture made from wood taken from sustainable forests. In some countries, products are stamped to indicate the sources of their raw materials.

Look out also for re-makes of classic twentieth-century designs (or buy originals second hand). The origins of much of today's furniture lie in the 1950s and 60s, when post-war designers introduced moulded and curvilinear forms – a good example being the modern version of the Arne Jacobsen Ant chair pictured as a dining set on page 83. Look for plywood re-makes (originals in particular are made from synthetic materials). Their purity of design makes them a stylish choice for the Zen home, as the simplicity of their form and structure is beautifully highlighted in a pale, pared-back setting.

OPPOSITE PAGE: A place that is easy to live in is more calming on the soul. This living area has low-level furniture, mixing a white sofa with warm woods and a shock of purple in the chaise longue.

Decorative

Decoration is a rare but essential aspect of the Zen interior – indeed Zen is a celebration of beautiful things. For maximum effect, introduce it sparingly through pieces of furniture placed with due thought into a simple setting. Against plain forms, we can enjoy the spendour and purity of detail these pieces have to offer.

Decorative furniture can range from the elaborate qualities in the curlicues of a wrought iron table and the grandeur of an antique French dresser, to the more down-to-earth charms of a driftwood coffee table set on castors or a plain white table with a central well of shingle and pebbles. This last can become a focal point at the heart of a sitting area – drawing us to the stones, which we can pick up and roll in the hand. (See pages 88-89 for details.)

BELOW: The majestic form of this gilded mirror is a stunning focal point in an all-white setting. The strong design is picked up in the decorative detail of the candle holders on the table.

Old with new

The Zen home is neither modern, nor traditional. It can be an eclectic environment that focuses on beauty, spirit, and function rather than fashion, rarity, or value.

Old pieces add a sense of history and continuity to our homes whether, as family heirlooms, they have a historical connection to us, or simply that the evidence of time has left its mark on the surface. Linked by a common aim, classic designs of excellence from the past, such as a Mackintosh chair, fit comfortably alongside late twentieth-century designs. In fact, the sharper images of modern furniture can provide a pleasing balance with the softer worn appearance of older pieces.

But before you race out to buy more furniture, new or old, it is worth assessing whether any items of furniture currently in your possession, could be customized to meet your present needs. Pieces of furniture can be given a new look with paint: try adding a muted natural hue, such as sea blue or taupe, then paint over with white or off-white and then when dry, sand away touches of paint to reveal the colour underneath and create a gently weathered appearance. A crackle glaze, applied between two coats of colour, lends an all-over texture, similar in appearance to the rugged look of bark or the worn feel of peeling paint.

All these treatments are good for adding character to new pieces of furniture or bringing colour to older pieces that have lost their appeal. Otherwise, re-upholster old and worn pieces of furniture or revitalize them with soft loose covers or a row of plump new cushions.

Utilitarian

There is often a temptation to divide the furniture
in our home: to put on show what we regard as
part of a decorative scheme, and to disguise or
even shut away the objects that we use rather
than look at. Most modern homes, for example,
have a television and stereo and a computer.
Instead of trying to deny their existence – by creating convoluted methods of storage that make
them difficult to access – we can accentuate their
modernity by setting them in isolation on a simple
table or cabinet, therefore, making them a part of
the general theme of our home. We can also draw
on the function of the room by furnishing a home
office area, for example, with strictly utilitarian
items. Rather than shying away from functional
forms, we instead embrace the purity of what they
have to offer and in so doing, derive pleasure from
the most ordinary aspects of everyday life. Look
for strong plain designs, items on wheels that
have a utilitarian feel, filing cabinets and other
office furniture. Co-ordinate materials and spray or
paint aberrant items to fit your design scheme.

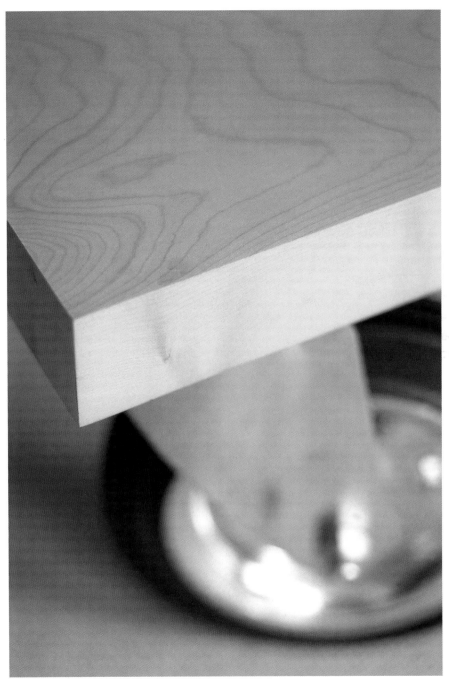

ABOVE: Utilitarian touches, such as the industrial appearance of this large chrome wheel can still be beautiful to look at, reflecting an honesty of design.

LEFT: The rich mellow tones of aged wood lend a sense of history to the home.

Painted table

A simple painted table brings natural elements into the home by utilizing a decorative inset of stones.

1 To make the table top, mark a square in the centre of the wood no larger than 30cm/12in across (the table shown in the photograph uses a central square of 8.5cm/3$^3/_8$in). To mark your square, draw two straight lines connecting diagonally opposite corners so that they cross in the centre. Measure from this central point out along each diagonal to the required size of your square and connect up. Using a jig-saw, cut away the central square to leave a hole in the table top.

2 To make the legs: drill a 17.5mm/$^5/_{16}$in hole in the centre of each leg piece. Slide the leg pieces onto the length of dowel positioning two at either end in a cross to form the legs. Making sure the dowel sits flush with the surface of each outer leg, glue in place using wood adhesive.

3 With the plywood lying face down, position the legs and draw around them as a guide. Remove the legs and drill screw holes using the outlines as a guide. Turn the plywood over and place it on top of legs, and using the drill holes, fix into position using the 25mm/1in screws.

4 Place the table base with legs attached upside down on the underside of the table top and screw together using four 5mm/$^4/_{16}$in screws along each side. Prime and undercoat the table, then sand down and fill where necessary. Paint the table with two coats of white eggshell and a coat of polyurethane varnish. Fill the recessed central square with the small stones and decorate the surface with a few pebbles.

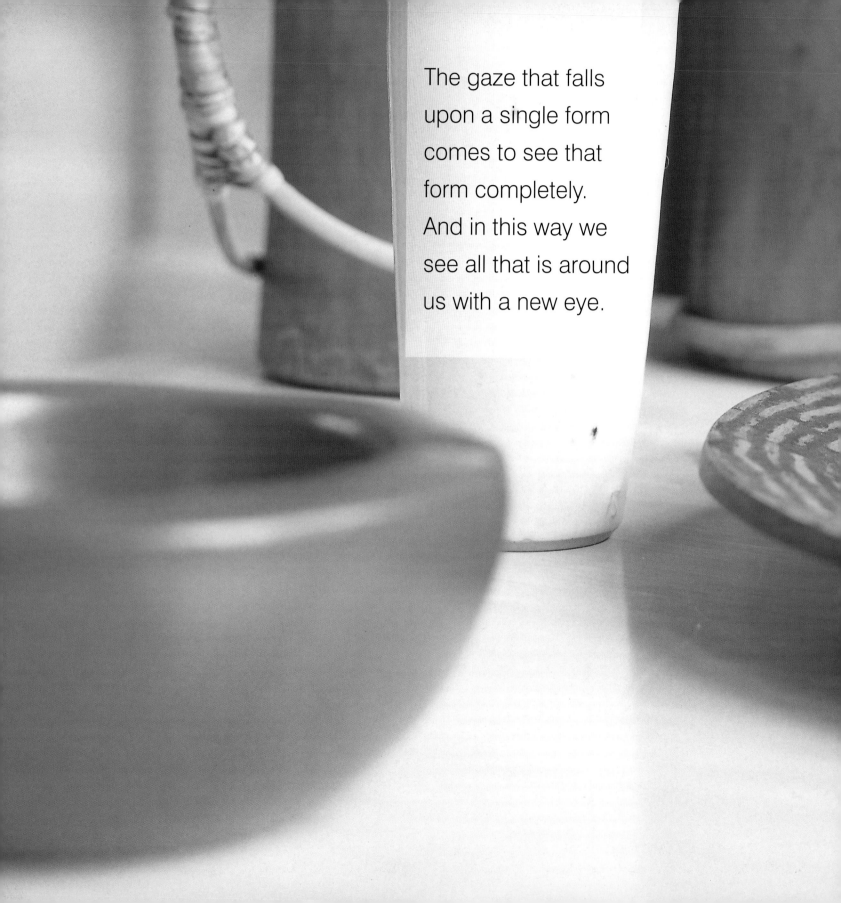

The gaze that falls
upon a single form
comes to see that
form completely.
And in this way we
see all that is around
us with a new eye.

details an individual spirit

We bring our spirit to our home through the design choices that we make. But it is in the details and the finishing touches that our true sense of self is expressed and our home becomes more of a personal space. Many houses have a similar layout and each item of furniture bears the presence of its maker. It is in the details we introduce that we personalize our homes and make them distinctly our own. Visits to craft stores, markets, junk shops and trips abroad can all yield unusual and interesting items, while browsing art shows and craft shops can yield unique finds of hand-crafted pieces, and creative use of practical and household items can incorporate them into your design scheme. Only when we add these final, individual touches, does it truly become our own space.

Everyday items have the potential to be used decoratively. Things that we normally pass over, should be looked at again, to see how they can be used to create interest and detail. It is important to use details sparingly for maximum effect. Don't rush this process, as it is often best to spend time in each room with the furnishings and decoration in place. This allows you to get to know each space intimately and understand what you can use; what, if anything, needs to be added and where. It may be that colour is required, or the furniture is too plain and would benefit from a hint of texture, or perhaps a rug laid on painted floorboards would add extra visual interest. Adding details to a space is an on-going organic process: until we introduce one element, we cannot be sure whether further dressing will be needed. Each piece should bring just the right accent and atmosphere to a space. Be sensitive to the changing light of the different seasons and augment the colours with flowers and accessories that vitalize the space – brightly coloured flowers might resonate perfectly in the sunshine of summer, but in the winter months, the exuberant greenness of a house plant could be more appealing and appropriate, reminding us of the fertility and colour of warmer seasons.

Adding detail is also about adding personality. It is these irreplaceable touches, created by and for us, which truly make our home unique – a shell found on a holiday, a picture painted by a friend, a home-made photo album, an old toy given to us in childhood. These personal items infused with memory allow us to connect with the past and bring soul into a home as well as making it a pleasure to look at.

OPPOSITE: A couple of delicate flowers in a small vase make the perfect simple detail.

The secret ingredient

ABOVE: So much enjoyment is found in a single stone. Use it as a secret ingredient in the home, from its mottled decorative qualities to the pleasure of rubbing your fingers over its smooth weathered surface.

RIGHT: The cleansing function of the sink is evoked in the graceful outlines and purity of shape.

Details provide the accent in a room. They shine out against the simplicity of the surroundings and change the rhythms of the room. As your eye roves around the room, it will come to stop at these small touches, that can carry as much visual interest as a large wooden dresser, or a bright coloured sofa. A wall that seems too plain can suddenly be transformed by the addition of a picture with colours that harmonize with the rest of the room.

And we come to appreciate the quality of these accents when they are used in isolation – a single vase on a shelf reveals more than a host of different shapes standing together which merge and become blurred and undefined. Similarly, a wall covered with different styled pictures and a mixture of different frames presents a confused vision, one in which our experience of the pictures themselves is lost. Avoid the urge to over-decorate – arguably, we find greater connection with a single stone that encourages us to pick it up and hold it than with a whole pile. When using details in the Zen home, the focus should always be on quality and not quantity.

The finishing touches

It is by attending to the details often overlooked in the decorative scheme that you can gain the most satisfaction. These are the finishing touches – the choice of light switch, the fine finger joints on the corner of a drawer or piece of furniture, or the moulding on the skirting boards. Door handles, for example, are one of the most common features in a house, and although small in size, they can have a tremendous visual impact. A plain row of floor to ceiling cupboards can be given a spark of vitality with small, silver handles that catch the light. Beyond appearance, we need to think about what they feel like to touch and how easy they are to use. From a run of plain fronted kitchen units comes the temptation to add embellishment, but simple touches that follow the clean lines of our surroundings can often have a more striking effect.

Finishing touches don't need to be obvious – we can adapt stones to form door handles, or attach fine pieces of slate to light pulls or keys left permanently in doors as a decorative touch. Locks, especially for internal doors, are similarly important for the way they catch our attention, we might wish to invest in solid looking traditional ones salvaged from old houses, thus bringing the past into our home.

We shape
clay into
a pot,
But it is the
emptiness
inside
That holds
whatever
we want.

Tao Te Ching

Most of us already have the kind of objects around us with which to complete the look of our home. We do not necessarily need to spend money, but simply divide what we want to have on show and what to store away.

To keep the look serene and uncluttered,,choose accessories with simple and elegant shapes. A stack of cream china or opaque glasses can become a decorative highlight when placed in a group. A large cream bowl in the middle of a dining table can be the only finishing touch that is required – every time we pass by we see the roundness of the bowl's shape against the surrounding landscape and are reminded of its inherent beauty. Rows of storage jars in a neutral kitchen with different coloured pasta, lentils or beans add welcome flashes of colour, or a row of utensils hanging from a bar lends subtle interest of shape. Similarly the strictly functional look of a bathroom with a white ceramic bath or basin can be softened and given points of interest with ornate chrome taps, either modern and sleek, or large Victorian or Edwardian style.

We can be creative with the most ordinary of items – the use of brown bags, decorated with photos from a recent holiday, become a charming display, and a joyful discovery for visitors, when hung on a wall as a personal memento. An arrangement of woven baskets in a line on the floor is an modest way of providing interesting texture. Ordinarily we might disregard them as run of the mill, but set against a simple backdrop they form a striking visual decoration.

ABOVE: The curves of the bowl sit in contrast to the lines in the wooden table.

BELOW: A row of mugs echoes the line of the shelf yet creates interest through repetition of shape.

Warmth and softness

The hard edges of furniture can be softened with a casual throw over a sofa or rolled linen napkins on a rectangular table. A pile of fluffy towels looks inviting against the straight lines of shelving, as does a fleecy rug on the floor beside the fire. Cushions in particular are our allies in comfort, especially when covered in warm oranges, reds and yellows. Mix layers of more luxuriant fabrics together in moderation such as wool, cashmere, suede, mohair, velvet and corduroy to heighten tactile sensations.

LEFT: The smallest detail still has impact. A line of drawn-thread work on white serviettes rolled inside fine chrome rings add a classic note to a table setting.

LEFT: Look for ways to inject subtle pattern into soft furnishings, such as this two-tone knitted cushion cover with bobble details.

OPPOSITE PAGE: Cushions and throws can make simple pieces of furniture more inviting.

97

Pictures

A large, single print or painting on a wall can provide the cohesive element that brings a room to life. On a large expanse of wall, a row of similarly styled pictures with matching frames can reinforce the symmetry of a room. The frames are important and should be selected to harmonize with the art they display, so make sure that the image is not overpowered by your choice of frame. Take a look at nature for inspiration and ideas: bamboo, driftwood, and twigs to form a frame; shells and pebbles for embedding into materials such as plaster of Paris for a frame (this can be bought in small bags). The possibilities are endless. If something can be securely fixed to a base, then it has the potential to make an interesting, and highly unique frame.

Experiment with creating your own pictures using natural materials. Place natural objects into a frame such as a row of pressed leaves or flowers for example. You could also match the picture to the frame. For larger objects you may need to use a box frame that has sufficient depth.

Mirrors are an essential decorative element of any home, not just for practical reasons, but in the way they reflect the light, opening up the area and increasing the feeling of space. Choose mirrors with frames that complement your interior design style.

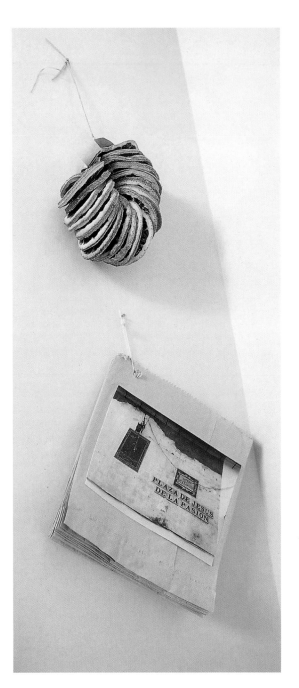

LEFT: A panel of snapshots is given uniformity by using black and white prints only.

ABOVE: Pictures do not have to be set in frames. Here a picture is attached and hung on a brown paper bag.

Flowers and plants

There is nothing to compare to the luscious delight of a vase of flowers. The colour, texture and scent bring life and vitality into our home and remind us of the overwhelming beauty of nature. In a room of neutral colours, the presence of rich blooms awakens the senses.

When arranging flowers, consider the receptacle, how the flower and vase work together, where the flowers are to be placed. Crystal clear water in a glass vase looks striking with a few single stems; flower heads floating in a shallow circular bowl make a attractive table centrepiece. In keeping with the Zen style of introducing the outdoors into the home, think about creating a living arrangement. This can be done easily with a crop of mustard or cress on a plate, grasses in pots or herbs such as sage, rosemary, lemon verbena and basil in bowls. Line up a row of them in interesting pots for a distinct table decoration at a dinner party, or place them in the centre of the kitchen table for you to admire as you use them. (See pages 100-101 for details.)

Plants can bring strong shapes and outlines to a room. Think of architectural plants with spiky shaped leaves that resonate against other outlines in the space. Make creative displays or foliage using mosses, twigs and pussy willow, and fronds of small palms or ferns.

RIGHT: A feast of floral texture and colour along the window ledge is given visual uniformity by being set in similar brushed chrome vases.

Mustard and cress table decoration

Liven up a kitchen area or create an unusual centrepiece for a dining table with a crop of fresh growing herbs.

YOU WILL NEED:

• **Large packets of mustard seeds and cress seeds**
• **White cotton wool in a roll**
• **Large tray or plate**
• **Large plastic bag (to cover plate)**
• **String**
• **Shallow dish**

1 Cut five small oblongs from the cotton wool and wet thoroughly with cold water. Arrange the cotton wool on the tray and sprinkle alternately with mustard seeds and cress seeds, using a mixture of both for the central piece. The seeds should cover the cotton wool but not be laid too thickly.

2 Place the seed tray into the plastic bag and tie the end with string ensuring there is enough air inside to give the seeds space to grow. Place the tray in a dark, warm cupboard.

3 After about two or three days when the seedlings are an inch high, remove the tray from the plastic bag and place in a light warm room. Add a little water if the cotton wool looks dry.

4 After a few days when the seedlings have grown a little higher, place them in a decorative shallow dish to use as a table arrangement. Alternatively, cut the tops of the sprouts and rinse under cold water before serving.

If we can leave behind all thoughts and words our minds can be open and free and our senses truly awakened.

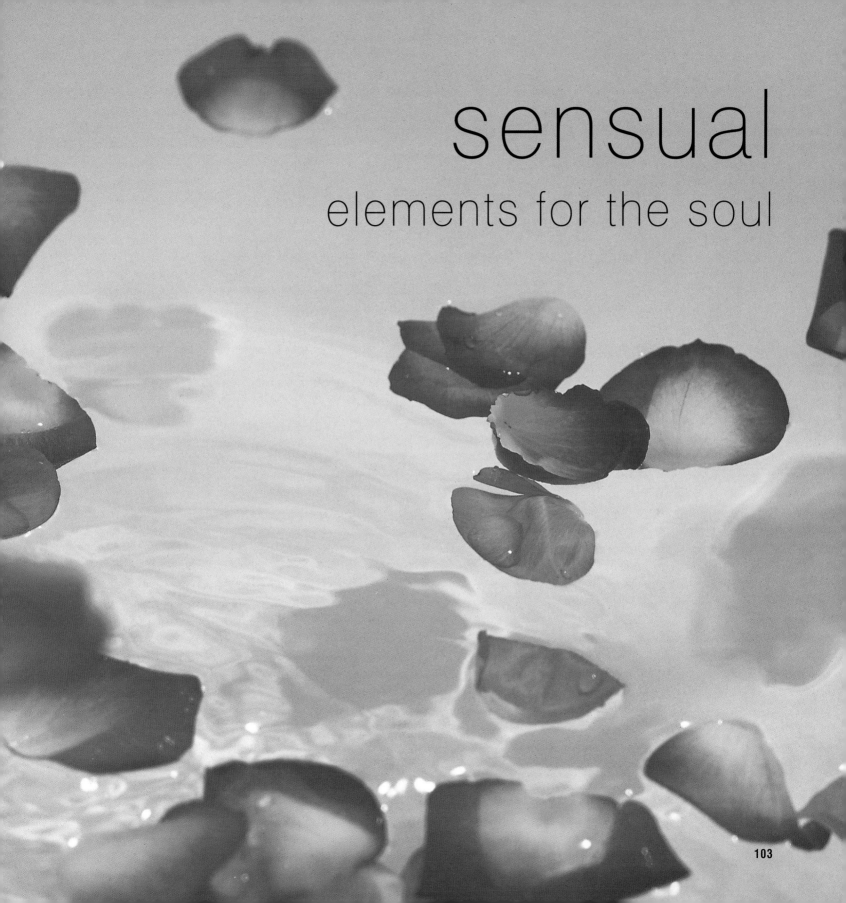

sensual
elements for the soul

By and large we think of our home as a visual place, and concern ourselves with the things we see and touch. For the home to become an environment that encourages relaxation and spiritual growth, it must stimulate all the senses, including smell, taste and sound. Unfortunately, this element of home decoration is often left unexplored. The sensual touch is a less tangible aspect which we might find hard to express in words, but feel deeply none the less. It lies in the smallest sensation, such as the smell of freshly ground coffee wafting through a room, the music of wind chimes on the garden porch, and the trickle of an indoor water fountain, or it can be found in something more enveloping such as the sound and heat of a crackling open fire. Experiences that flow through us and to which we respond intuitively arouse our senses in the simplest ways, helping us to relax. In many ways, the things we can introduce to transform our living space into a sensual home are the easiest and most effortless aspects of home decorating.

BELOW: LEFT: The aroma of ripe fruit stimulates the sense of smell and awakens the memory how it tastes.

If we bring out the sensual side of our home, we add depth to the experiences of living there. Fragrances can instill a sense of calm and invigorate every cell in our body. The sound of gently running water induces feelings of contentment. Candle and firelight are less harsh to the eye than artificial light and promote mental relaxation.The sensual side can even come from the things we do, by acknowledging the importance of setting time aside to concentrate on ourselves. Moderation is the key. Delicate smells and sounds that touch the senses are better than those that overpower them.

OPPOSITE: Simple pleasures such as scenting bath water with herbs and bath salts encourage complete relaxation.

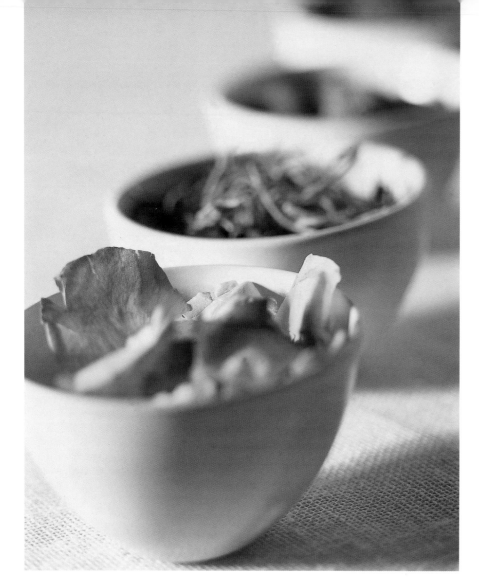

Scent

Small bowls of dried flowers or herbs can be used to imbue a bedroom with a light scent that enhances the sense of comfort. In a bathroom, a fresh, energizing aroma can reinforce our connection with the idea of cleansing and starting each day anew. Small stones or wooden shapes infused with fragrance provide a decorative textural display as well.

Aromatherapy is well recognized for its re-vitalizing properties. Essential oils can be used to promote well-being through massage and bathing. Lavender, for instance, is good for soothing anxiety and stress, bergamot is energizing, while geranium is uplifting, giving the spirit a boost. There are several ways that essential oils can be used around the house to release a subtle health-improving scent, particularly when placed near a gentle source of heat. Add a few drops of oil to a bowl of dried flowers or potpourri, padded clothes hangers or drawer liners, light bulbs, a specially designed oil burner, or a saucer of water placed above a radiator.

ABOVE: Use a line of bowls of dried flowers and herbs to decorate a windowsill or mantlepiece .

RIGHT: Essential oils have properties that are good for the body and mind. A collection of stones imbued with a few drops of your favourite oil bring freshness to a room.

There is no better tonic to our sense of smell than the presence of fresh herbs. Whether or not you have a garden, bring the outside in by growing a variety of herbs in pots or place them on a windowsill. They don't have to stay in the kitchen – a small rosemary plant by the side of a workplace, for example, can enhance memory and stimulate creativity through its aroma.

For night-time relaxation, incense sticks or essential oil burners with a few drops of sandalwood or camomile used sparingly around the bedroom, can induce a restful night's sleep.

TOP: Light a few incense sticks in the evening to help you unwind.

ABOVE: Look for blooms with a distict fragrance, such as the a couple of glorious springtime hyacinths.

LEFT: An indoor lavender plant releases a soft aroma that goes almost unnoticed but has positive effects none-the-less.

Water

Water is the ultimate symbol of purity, and in its presence we feel cleansed and refreshed; from a simple glass of water to an invigorating shower. Water in the home also has aesthetic and calming qualities. One way to promote these qualities is through decorative displays – a bowl of water with flower petals or floating candles, or a glass container of water, pebbles, and greenery brought in from the garden, can remind us of nature by introducing colour and texture from outdoors.

Water is also about sound and movement – think of the rhythmic beating of waves against the shore, or the trickling water of a mountain stream. Listening to moving water has the same affect on us as watching flames crackling and leaping in a fireplace – both seem to hold us mesmerized. There is something inexplicably delightful about the sound of water, and this can be created indoors by placing a small water pump in a medium sized bowl of water. Alternatively, you might wish to be more adventurous and make your own fountain, drawing in other elements of nature as well. (See pages 114-115 for details.)

Water flowing over us, or hydrotherapy, is another way we can enjoy the magical qualities of water. It can relax or stimulate the body depending on the pressure and temperature, improving circulation, relieving joint and muscular pain and soothing the sympathetic nervous system. If you are about to give your bathroom an overhaul, you might like to consider putting in a power shower or whirlpool for their massaging properties, or a deep Japanese tub, which, having a smaller surface area than a conventional bath, retains its heat for longer.

ABOVE: Trails of moss are set against bamboo, water and stones to create a sensual indoor water garden.

RIGHT: The sound of water is one of the most relaxing elements you can introduce in the home.

OPPOSITE: It is easy to make a miniature water fountain. Just place a small pump in a bowl, cover it with pebbles and add water.

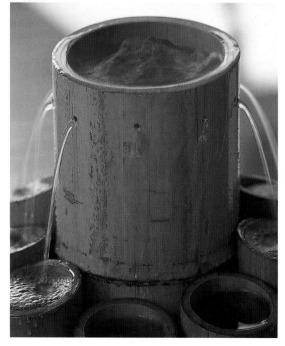

Pebbles on the riverbed, Wavering: Clear water. Zen Haiku

Ambience

Our home contains its own natural atmosphere, but at certain times we might wish to impose a stronger mood on a space in order to evoke a more dramatic atmosphere.

Candlelight is the most evocative way we can alter the ambience of a room. It is the most basic way of creating illumination, and yet it brings so many elements into play. There is the light itself which, depending on the quantity or size of the candles, can be bright and glorious, or dim and restful which is perfect for moments when we just want to sit and do nothing. The flickering flame and the patterns it creates, provide a peaceful and ever-changing sight for the eyes. Then there is the fragrance that we can bring into play by burning aromatic candles, or placing a tea light in a special oil burner. These infuse the room with a gentle aroma that can have a subtle effect on mood and atmosphere.

We can change the qualities of the light by the way we set out the candles – place them in clusters of intense light, or on the floor around a fireplace to complement the glow of a fire. If we put candles inside a lantern or a simple glass or vase, we can throw out a variety of different patterns into the room. Similarly, candles floating in water create an undulating sensation of light which can be used to form a soft centrepiece for a dining table, or on a table outside on a still summer evening.

LEFT: Tea lights set around a bath allow you to forget about the rest of your surroundings and concentrate your thoughts solely on the pleasure of bathing.

RIGHT: Different ways of displaying candles can change the mood they set. Dark textural holders provide an earthy balance.

BELOW: Nothing compares to the allure of a real log fire. It provides a central focus for any room, while the sound, smell, colours and heat refresh the senses. Add a sprig of rosemary to dying embers to release its uplifting fragrance.

RIGHT: Large candles with more than one wick make superb decoration in themselves. Place them on the floor and allow the silhouettes to speak for themselves.

Time for yourself

Humans are by nature social creatures and yet, we still crave peace and solitude. Spending time alone in reflection is an important part of spiritual recuperation and keeping physically healthy. Being alone is not the same as loneliness, for being alone on a regular basis can have positive effects – less stress, quality time doing what you enjoy the most, a chance to catch up with how you feel about your life, and sorting out priorities. In Zen, this is known as 'cultivating emptiness' and 'doing nothing', both of which can help us to clear out the mind clutter and relieve stress.

Unfortunately, there is an attitude in today's society that we should be constantly busy, and we often feel guilty if we do not live up to this. 'Doing nothing' simply means that we keep all activity to a minimum while we reflect and recharge our batteries. This can take many forms – spending time with pets, and making time to do things we enjoy such as hobbies, cooking, and gardening. These moments of pleasure can provide the greatest source of contentment and relaxation.

Give time over for the occasional lie-in and breakfast in bed, or for curling up on a sofa and engrossing yourself in a good book. Pleasure comes from pampering yourself – the relief of hopping into a nice hot bath after a hard day's work is an experience most of us relish, especially when you can soak in bath preparations packaged in exquisite bottles, or a scattering of rose petals. Even a handful of salt or a few droplets of oil added to bathwater can provide relief to the nervous system and tired muscles as they are absorbed directly through the skin into the bloodstream. Whatever helps you relax is the key to restoring balance between mind, body and soul.

RIGHT: Taking time to pamper ourselves is an important part of our daily or weekly rituals. Thinking only of ourselves for a short white reconnects us to our own needs and feelings.

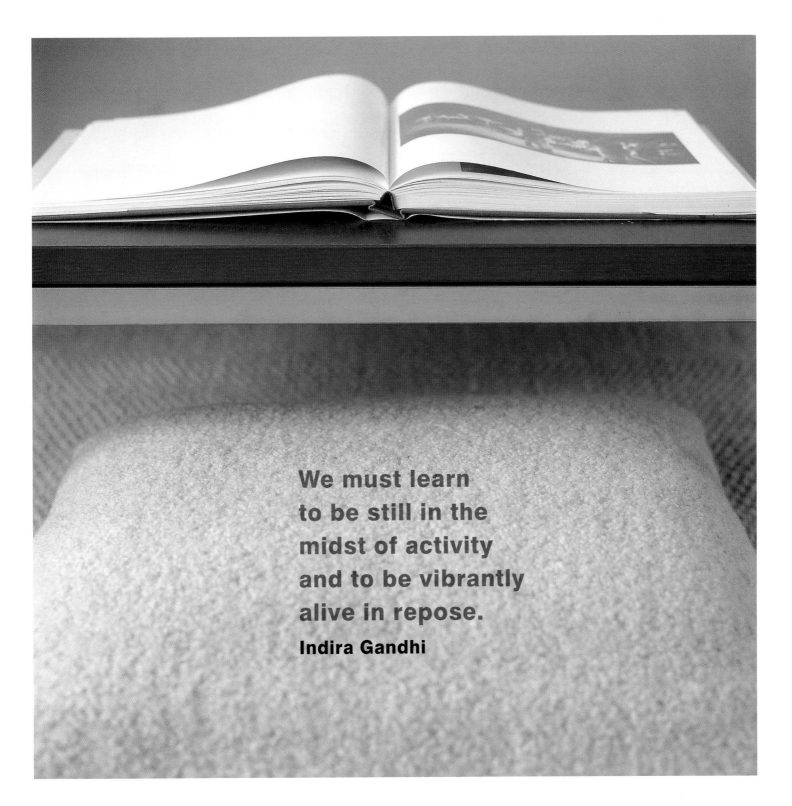

**We must learn
to be still in the
midst of activity
and to be vibrantly
alive in repose.**

Indira Gandhi

Water fountain

The sound of running water combined with the colour and texture of natural elements, evokes the spirit of the great outdoors.

NB: The instructions refer to 'chambers' in the length of bamboo, these are indicated on the outside of the bamboo by the circular grooves around the pole at various intervals along the length. When measurements for 'chambers' are given, simply measure from these grooves along the outside of the bamboo.

1 To make the central section, cut a 64cm/25¹/₄in length of 15cm/6in diameter bamboo. You will need to adjust where you cut this section from the piece of bamboo to ensure the top has a 14cm/5¹/₂in chamber and the bottom has a chamber of at least 6cm/2³/₈in. Using a 13mm/¹/₂in drill bit, drill a hole down through the centre of the chambers to take the copper pipe. Trim the pipe so that 10cm/4in extends into the top chamber and 3cm/1¹/₄in extends down into the bottom chamber. Place it in position and use metal filler at the base of the top chamber to create a water-tight seal. Allow to dry. Using a 15mm/⁹/₁₆in drill bit, drill a hole in the side of the bamboo 1cm/¹/₂in up from the base. Push a little of the flexible hose through and fit it onto the end of the copper pipe (the other end will be attached to the pump). Create a sloping top by trimming down to 2cm/³/₄in lower at the outside edge.

2 Cut the lengths of bamboo (measurements below) to form the ten pieces for the outer section, making sure that the top chambers are no longer than 20cm/7⁷/₈in. To help the water flow easily, cut the top of each piece at an angle so that they slope gently towards the outside edge.

7cm/2³/₄in diameter pieces:
1 x 48cm/19in; 2 x 49cm/19¹/₃in; 2 x 50.5cm/19³/₄in; 1 x 53cm/20⁷/₈in

5cm/2in diameter pieces:
1 x 53cm/20⁷/₈in; 2 x 54cm/21¹/₄in; 1 x 55cm/21⁵/₈in

Measure 22cm/8³/₄in up from the bottom of each piece (there should be a complete chamber on every piece above this line) and make a mark on each side. Drill a hole through these two points. Lay the pieces on the floor arranged in order of height with the shorter pieces in the centre. Cut a 2.5m/8ft1¹/₂in length of galvanized wire and thread each piece onto it through the holes.

3 Mark a line around the top of the central section, 60.5cm/23⁷/₈in from the bottom. Position the bamboo pieces on the wire around the central section and tie in place leaving a small opening at the back close to the exit for the flexible hose. Mark the centre position of each pole along the horizontal line on the central bamboo piece, remove the outer section and drill a hole through each of these marks. To make the bamboo cuff for the bowl, measure the circumference of the plastic bowl and divide by 1.5cm/⁵/₈in (to give you the number of short bamboo lengths you will need). Cut this number of pieces from the 1.5cm/⁵/₈in diameter lengths of bamboo to the height of the bowl plus 2cm/³/₄in. Drill a hole near the top and bottom of each piece and then thread onto the galvanized wire as before.

4 Place the central section in the centre of the bowl. Wrap the outer section around this ensuring the pieces line up underneath the holes drilled in the central section. Twist the ends of the wire together to fix the outer section in place. Wrap the cuff around the outside of the bowl and fix it in place in the same way. Trim off any excess. Pull the flexible hose through the outer section and connect it to the pump. Place the pump in the bowl with the stones in the bottom to fix the fountain in place. Set the fountain in position and plug into the mains supply, then fill the bowl with water. Switch on the pump – as the fountain fills up you will need to add more water (the pump should always be covered with water). Decorate the base with more stones. For a further decorative touch, set a couple of spare pieces of bamboo around the fountain and place a water plant and some moss inside.

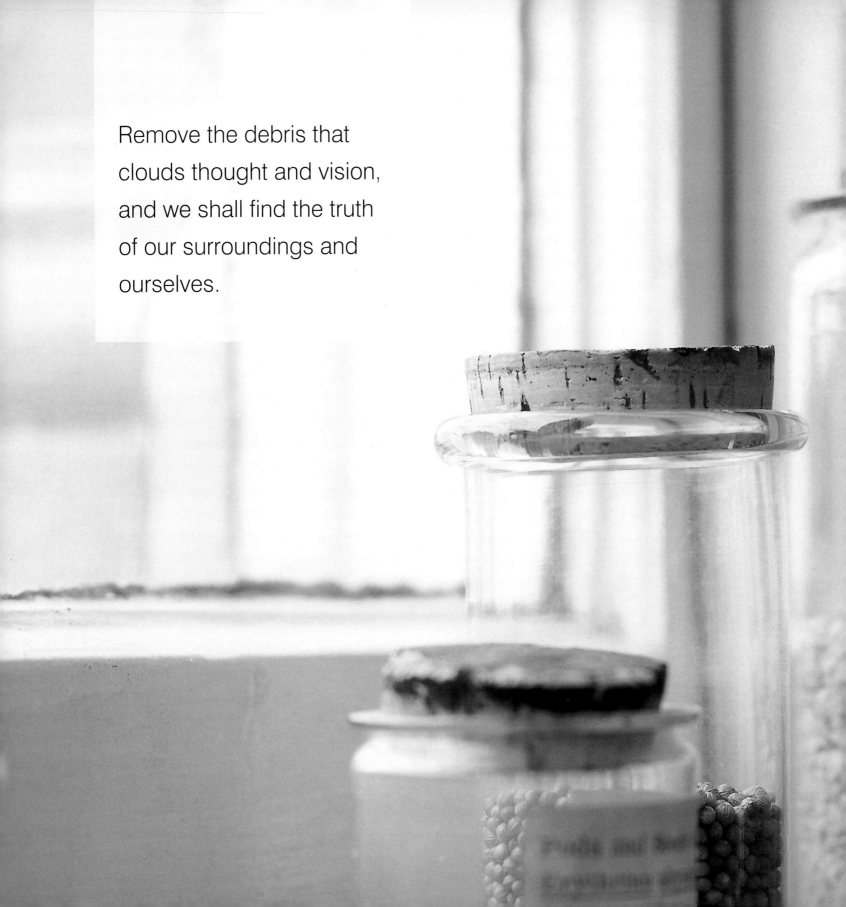

Remove the debris that
clouds thought and vision,
and we shall find the truth
of our surroundings and
ourselves.

storage

uncluttering the mind

Our state of mind benefits infinitely from an ordered home that is free from the chaos of unnecessary possessions. That does not mean stripping the home bare, but rather being selective and giving everything a designated place to which it is always returned. It is through these selective decisions rather than impulsive clear-outs that we are able to keep a sense of self and our life's journey. Think how wonderful it would be to return each day to an organized environment and the atmosphere of calm we would find there.

In some respects, a streamlined interior brings its own sense of orderliness; the discipline of straight lines and simple forms provides a cohesive frame that helps to tidy the view. But if we are to feel completely comfortable, the Zen home must be able to cope with the disorder of life. There is little joy to be had from living in a place where we must be obsessively tidy to preserve the harmony. But too much clutter becomes oppressive, reduces the feeling of space and is a distraction from other sights and sensations in the home. If we want to maintain the feeling of openness, then we need good storage systems.

Storage provides a compromise between the need for possessions and the need for space. It is about organization as well as tidiness so that we can accomplish tasks easily and without fuss. Efficient storage is not just about being able to clear things from view, but also about finding a way to streamline the appearance of objects and items – for in some cases, we may want to have things within reach, particularly in a kitchen or bathroom. Thinking about storage involves establishing systems for keeping the clutter level as low as possible, such as getting into the habit of recycling newspapers and magazines in regular

batches, rather than allowing them to collect into unwieldy piles. And, of course, we must also consider how to meld our storage systems with the theme of simplicity so that practical solutions become style solutions as well.

Successful storage needs to be well planned. Items that we need on a day-to-day basis must be close-at-hand and within easy reach; things that are rarely required can be stowed in less accessible places such as in the loft, cellar or garage. Try to divide your storage system into sections and organize the contents accordingly. Many shelves in a cupboard, for example, give you plenty of space to store the contents making it easier to see what you've got – by comparison, two or three shelves piled high with items mean you have to sort through everything to find what you're after, and they are more likely to become untidy. Consider what needs to be stored and try and adapt the system accordingly. A wardrobe or area for clothes, for example, needs a variety of fittings – a rail for hanging, shelves for your collections of sweaters and shoes, and perhaps a series of cubby holes in which to place small items or a run of pull out baskets so you can see what you've got at a glance.

ABOVE: Storage can be as much about display as hiding things away. Here a folding chair is stored away from the floor space by a hook on the wall.

OPPOSITE: Simple storage ideas impose order on the most unruly possessions and keep surroundings uncluttered. A neat line of shoes offers decorative simplicity and provides visual balance to the long bookshelf above.

119

Out of sight

RIGHT: A set of drawers can be a useful as well as decorative piece of furniture, allowing you to hide the things that you need to be able to access on a regular basis.

Storage units that seem to disappear into our surroundings, hiding our possessions completely from view, provide the most discreet solution. Cupboards are one of the most essential furniture items in our home because they can easily be adapted to fit with the style of the surroundings, and they can be fitted with shelves or hanging rails, thus providing an almost limitless option in terms of what you can store inside them. Those cupboards that can be incorporated into the structure are best, especially when finished with flat, plain doors and painted in the same colour as the rest of the room so they can melt into the surroundings. Making changes to the structure of a room can provide a prime opportunity to create spaces for built-in cupboards, but when this is not possible, look for dead space that can be converted without imposing on the openness of a room. Areas beneath stairways are perfect for cupboards. Alcoves, too, are good for both cupboards and sets of drawers, although in small rooms you need to make sure that they won't be too overbearing.

Consider encroaching a little on the space of a room by building a row of cupboards along one wall. They don't necessarily need to be very deep – a long hallway that ends in a blank wall can be adapted successfully in the same way. In some situations, cupboards can even serve to streamline irregularities – the line of an ugly box around pipes can be extended along a wall to form a cupboard, creating a stronger, more solid shape that looks as though it's supposed to be there.

RIGHT: Deep drawers are ideal for storing bulky items, such as sweaters and bedding.

Space beneath a bed is ideal for storage – it doesn't affect the atmosphere of a room and the space itself cannot be used for anything else. Cupboards or drawers built into the bed frame extend the outlines of the piece of furniture itself. Where space (and room for storage) is at a premium, a bed set higher than normal, can offer greater capacity for stowing things away. Alternatively, some form of box on wheels which can be pulled out from under the bed, also works well. Storage boxes mounted on castors are available in a wide range of styles and can be used in a variety of settings, at the side or beneath a work table, in a simple row against a wall, or even as an alternative to kitchen units, set beneath a work surface.

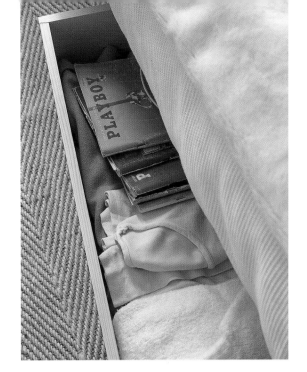

LEFT: Space beneath a bed is rarely noticed and often unused, yet makes an ideal place for an additional storage system.

BELOW: An alternative take on kitchen units, these wheel-out deep boxes are designed to fit beneath worksurfaces.

LEFT: The kitchen trolley is an essential piece of open-plan storage, that itself can be stored away when not in use.

121

Dual purpose

To retain as much space as possible we can look for storage solutions that combine more than one function – in place of two items of furniture, we have only one. This helps to keep areas clear and simple, as well as lessen the demands storage makes on our home. A low chest of drawers, for example, might be used in a living room as a coffee table, a tall sturdy box or chest could also work well as seating (especially useful in small rooms) or, if the right height, it could be utilized as a bedside table.

A panel behind a bed can be set a little distance from the wall to create a storage area behind – the panel functions as a bed head while at the same time providing the frame for a cupboard system.

Shelving

No home can survive without shelving and their geometric form works particularly well in pared-down living spaces. They can be painted in the same colour as the background for minimal impact or in a contrasting colour to create a sharp accent. Alternatively, the colour and pattern of natural materials, such as wood, can be used to introduce a streak of soft colour in a pale space.

Consider how the shelving might be placed for structural effect as well as storage, as a counter-point to the vertical lines of an area. A large expanse of wall, for example, seems to be even longer when set with one elegant shelf that extends the entire length of the plain. Keep the shelves as simple as possible to accentuate their

linear quality. Shelving in alcoves provides a set of clean, rigid lines which unify the objects stored there. Look for ways to incorporate additional shelving in unexpected places – a single shelf running beneath kitchen units for example, provides slim, barely noticeable, space for books and small items of crockery. We can also adapt the idea of shelving to other angular means of storage – a set of simple square boxes set in a row upon the wall can bring a sense of order to the mix of objects placed within. (See pages 126-127 for details.)

Simple displays on shelving provide a striking contrast to the straight lines of their form – a curved silhouette of a vase, three simple elegant pictures in matching frames or a surge of colour from a few flowers. Alternatively, we can use everyday objects to add colour and texture – the spines of books, rows of vertically stored magazines, a run of identical glass storage jars coloured by their contents. In keeping with the general Zen approach to the home, try to remove unnecessary objects by making thoughtful selections that form a striking visual impact against the surroundings.

ABOVE: Shelves are the easiest way to give cohesive form to an eclectic mix of possessions.

LEFT: A tall stack of built-in drawers provides striking visual symmetry as well as a natural recess a the side that could be used for a dressing table or further storage.

Storage as decoration

As with shelving, some storage systems can bring decorative qualities to a space. A chest of drawers, for example, with fine detailing or painted in a muted shade which harmonizes with the pale colour scheme, can become a simple focus in a room. Traditionally used in the bedroom, chests of drawers can work equally well in a hallway, as well as in a general living space. Unusual choices of furniture bring a personal touch too – a filing cabinet, sprayed white or ivory looks stunning in any space (not just a work area), old pieces, such as a wide wooden plans chest with shallow drawers, can provide an interesting contrast to modern pieces in a room.

RIGHT: Storage facilities can look chic, as demonstrated by the sleek metal filing cabinets, and desk that can also stand as a shelf unit for displaying artefacts.

OPPOSITE LEFT: A modern take on a classic idea. The Shaker-style peg rail enables you to display attractive utensils and kitchen essentials close at hand.

OPPOSITE RIGHT: The purity of white china and collection of drinking glasses lend a simple decorative quality to a kitchen.

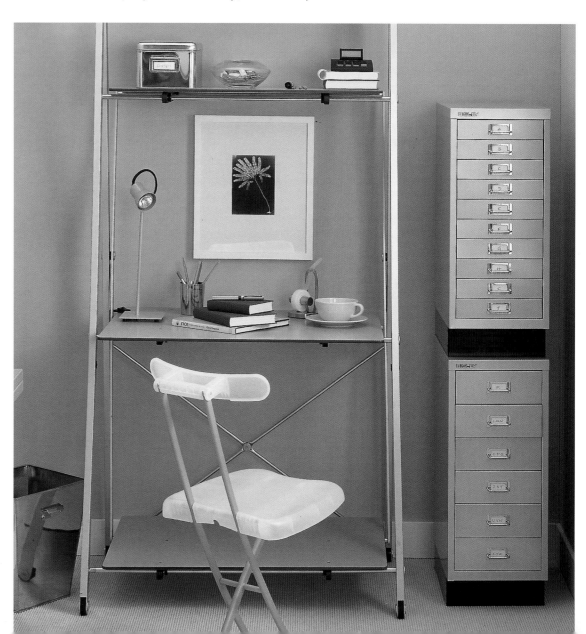

We can choose storage which allows the objects themselves to become decorative – we can show off the shapes and texture of crockery in a glass fronted cupboard, framed by the outline of the doors. Large plastic-lidded bins which contain the chaotic shapes of different items allow subtle shades, shapes and texture to show through. Even ordinary magazine racks, in wood or clear plastic, bring regularity and shape to the objects stored there.

Look for more creative solutions which can be inexpensive to put together – a row of brown or white carrier bags on a shelf or set on the floor along a wall, hide the objects stored within, and create strong shapes (they can also be replaced easily when they become tired and crumpled). Similarly, a stack of storage boxes, in soft shades of grey, muted brown or pure white, become a strong decorative motif that reflects the symmetry of the structure.

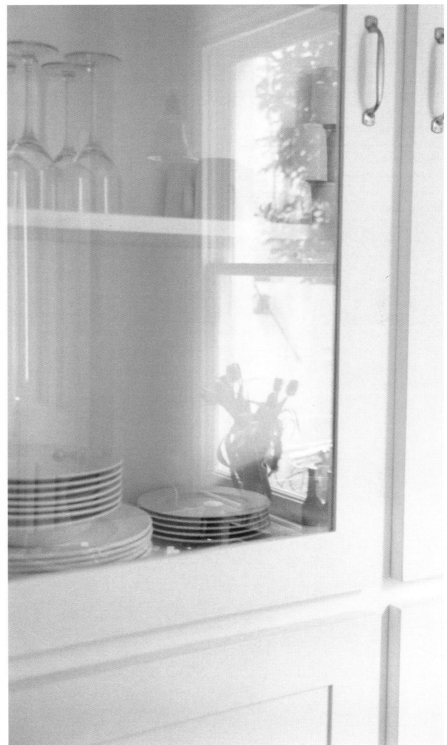

Wall boxes

Strong lines and soft colour provide streamlined regularity for household clutter.

YOU WILL NEED:

(for each box)

- **Four 100 x 230 x 15mm/4 x 9 x $\frac{1}{2}$in pieces of wood or medium density fibreboard (MDF)**
- **Twelve 2cm/$\frac{3}{4}$in nails**
- **Hammer**
- **Sandpaper**
- **Woodfiller**
- **Primer and undercoat**
- **Coloured eggshell for top coat**
- **Polyurethane varnish**
- **Paintbrushes**
- **Two picture hooks**

1 Place the short ends of the wooden pieces together to form a square box using three nails along each side to fix firmly in place.

2 Fill any holes with wood filler and sand the surface of the box to achieve a smooth finish.

3 Paint a coat of primer and a coat of undercoat on the inside and outside of the box. Allow the box to dry thoroughly between applications.

4 Apply two coats of coloured eggshell. When dry, apply one coat of polyurethane varnish to protect the surface of the box. Fix picture hooks in place at either side along the top of the back of the box. Hang all three boxes by using a spirit level to mark a vertical line on the wall for positioning. Set the boxes about 10cm/4in apart, hammer nails into the wall and hang the boxes in place.

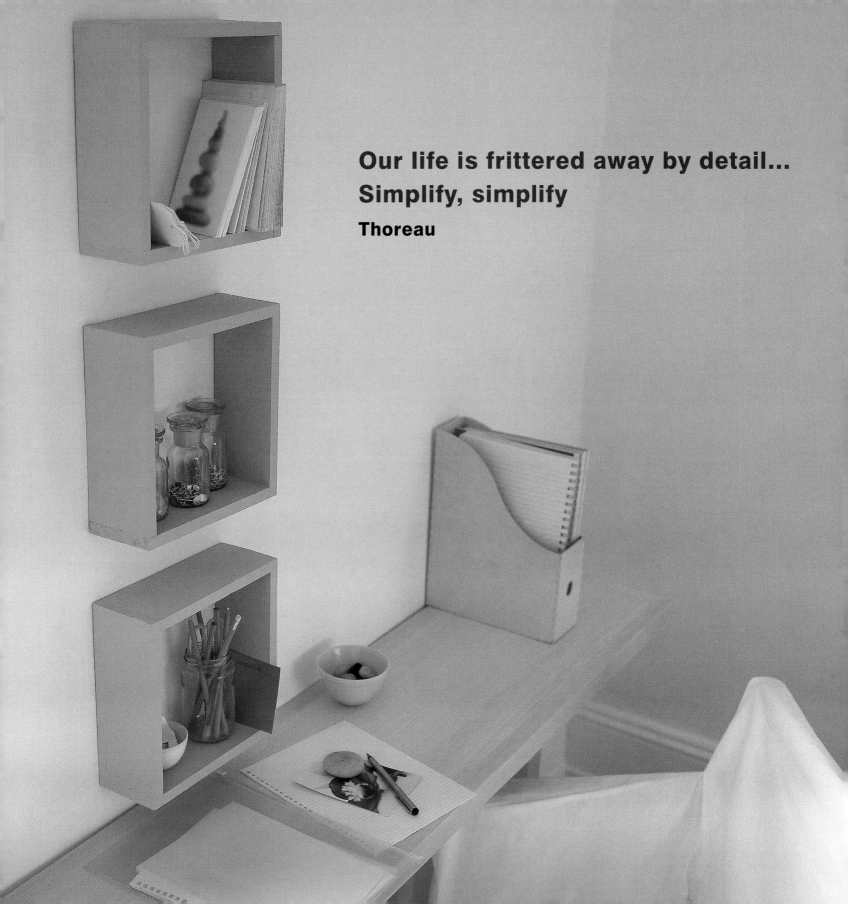

Our life is frittered away by detail...
Simplify, simplify

Thoreau

Only through thought and contemplation can
we find effortless liberation.

putting the look together
defining your style

Achieving a sense of balance between the many elements that go into making our home a peaceful one, is not something that happens by chance. A home that responds to the needs of the soul as well as the person, is one that has to be created through understanding those needs and finding ways to provide for them. We are all different, and we all have a different idea of what our ideal space for relaxing and living in should be like. And ultimately, the choices we make must be those that feel right for us and come from the heart.

Only by careful thought and consideration can we create a space that works well, is inviting and effortless to spend time in. When planning ideas, we need to take a holistic approach, considering all the elements of a space – the structure, the quality of light, how we use a room, the pervading atmosphere, furnishings and colour – to ensure they work together cohesively. This is important whatever the scale of change we are contemplating – altering the treatment of a window, for example, will cause a shift in balance in a room, so we need to be aware of all the different elements and how they will interact with one another to create a successful scheme. Our plan must also take on board the budget we have available and look for ways to adapt our ideas within this. Structural alterations are the most significant changes that we will make and need to be carefully thought out in consultation with a builder, or if the budget allows, an architect, to ensure that they will not have a negative impact on the soundness of the building's overall structure. Put together a plan as

this can be a useful guide when making decisions, as it allows you to see the elements in place. This can help narrow down the options, giving you a feel for what will and won't work in a particular room or space.

That is not to say that our plan for a room should be set in stone. We need to be flexible and willing to adapt to happy accidents or changes of heart that happen along the way. A home is something which evolves over time and we need to be prepared to work slowly, going back to the space in question as it takes shape and assessing how different aspects are working, adjusting our ideas to suit where necessary. An unusual item of furniture we come across and simply have to have, the discovery of a wonderful piece of fabric, a painting we fall in love with – all kinds of elements can alter our notion of how we see a finished space. And indeed, it is these aspects that can't be planned for which give our home its unique stamp of individuality.

Teachers open the door, but you must enter by yourself.

Chinese Proverb

OPPOSITE: A balance between simplicity and pattern, colour and neutrality, striking features and discreet detail, has been achieved in this bedroom to create a clean look that retains a sense of warmth and coziness.

The basic structure

The shell of your home is the basic building block from which all other possibilities emerge. While it sets the scene for everything that is to follow and provides the potential for change, conversely, it also determines the extent to which change is possible. Removing walls to create an open-plan area may not be the only solution, or the only one available. A large hallway running through the centre of the house, for example, may be the key to connecting spaces. By creating open doorways, or enlarging the openings, we link all the spaces together without losing the privacy of individual rooms. When thinking about the structure you also need to address storage issues, as structural alterations might allow for in-built storage units to be added at little extra cost.

If you are planning structural changes, then you will probably require professional expertise and planning. Even here, you need to be clear about your own vision for the space – it is easy to get caught up in the excitement of someone else's stunning ideas without considering how they will really work for you. Always refer back to your own plan to make sure that your needs will be met by the new layout. An efficient layout is essential for the Zen home. Aesthetics are important, but will count for nothing if the ergonomics of a room or area are not geared to your specific needs. The simplest decision, such as the height of a work station table and the relative position of a set of shelves above it can be just as crucial as the entire planning of a kitchen or bathroom.

But you don't just need to think of structure in terms of major changes. You can breathe new life and freshness into a space in much simpler ways. Removing woodwork from walls, such as dado rails and wainscoting, can have a dramatic effect on streamlining the appearance of a space. Think too about things you can change – perhaps there are built-in cupboards in alcoves which are too imposing for the space, but replacing these with open shelving may help lighten up the area. Revealing the floorboards and painting them in a pale colour helps increase the feeling of openness and space, while exchanging fussy window treatments for plain white blinds will accentuate the shape of the window and heighten its potential. Even the simple step of painting a room white can have a dramatic effect in terms of uncluttering the appearance of a room.

Inspiration

Very few ideas occur in isolation – we are influenced by everything around us and the images we see filter into our brain and are recalled, often without realizing, as a spark which stimulates our own creativity. Inspiration can be found in all manner of objects and visual references. The accidental colour combination of a flower against a backdrop, the colours in a holiday snap shot of a foreign landscape, the shapes and forms in a painting, a favourite jacket, even the packaging of a particular commodity might be just the colour you had in mind for your walls. If you collect all the visual sources together, you can begin to build up a picture of the kinds of shades, textures, patterns and combinations that you like.

Most of us find it hard to visualize how a scheme will look in the three dimensions of an actual room. Often, it's not until you see something that you can know if it will work. Interiors magazines and books are a valuable source of ideas for your home interior. Looking at how other homes have been put together can help clarify your own feelings about what you do and don't like, as well as suggesting ways in which you might adapt your own space, from colour to structural solutions.

They are also an excellent resource in terms of locating where to buy certain items. However, in looking at other people's homes you should also be wary. You need to view them as inspiration, let them lead you off down a particular avenue, rather than using them as a blueprint for your own living space. Lifting complete schemes is rarely successful, think instead of interpreting what you see and translating it into something that will be unique to your own home.

LEFT: Nature provides a wealth of inspiration. You can use it as a source for colours, patterns and texture, and well as using natural objects directly in the home.

Planning your ideas

OPPOSITE: Gather together pictures, magazine cuttings, fabrics, and paint swatches as a starting point for putting ideas together.

BELOW: It's a good idea to make a scaled-down plan of a room or space to help you look at how pieces of furniture will work within an area.

Having gathered an array of inspiring pictures, swatches and samples, you can begin to formulate a general vision for your interior space. Even if you are working on just one room it is worth considering the home as a whole – the impact of one room is changed by the atmosphere of another, the view we see ahead, the colour we leave behind.

Making a storyboard

Collect all the different swatches and scraps that you like and perhaps start a peg board to which you can clip them and begin painting a picture of ideas. At the inspiration stage it is a good idea to be as open as possible and refrain from editing your selection until you come to put your plan together. It is also helpful to gather as many catalogues as possible which can be referred to when making decisions about the final scheme.

Drawing up a scaled plan of a room is always worth the effort – even more so in functional spaces such as kitchens and bathrooms. Make scaled shapes of pieces of furniture you already have to see how they might be arranged in the space. As you work on your plan, keep going back to questions of how each space is used, and what objects are needed to make it more efficient. You might also consider trying out particular areas by mocking up the layout to check that your plan really will work in the way you envisage – for example, is there enough space between a bed and a cupboard or will it be too cramped.

Think too about the focus of a room – it may be structural, such as a large arched window, or defined by an area of colour or an architectural feature such as a fireplace, and therefore we need to keep other elements simple so as not to compete with this. With fabric swatches at hand, you can also consider how different textures and patterns might be balanced in a room – lightness at the window, warmth and comfort for a sofa. Look for ways in which you can introduce simple decorative elements too.

force of nature

Artist Jonathan Cook's observations evolve into original, confronting images of the natural world and the animal kingdom.

Paints and materials

RIGHT: Different swatches of wallpaper and materials for a bedroom. By comparing and contrasting, you will be able to narrow down your selection until you find exactly the right combination.

No matter how accurate the paint charts, paint colours never seem to quite work in the way we expect. The amount of colour in a room intensifies the shade, while different times of the day and the quality of light will also influence the finished look. The only safe way is to experiment. Use a length of lining paper (or the back of an old roll of wallpaper) the height of your room. Paint it in the colour you are considering and then hang it in the room. Move the sample to different areas and at different times of day so you can really see how the colour changes in the room. The paint type can also affect the quality of the colour. Gloss finishes can be reflective and stand out in simple surroundings – if you want to accentuate the lines on the floor boards, gloss paint may be just what you need. On the other hand, matt paints such as emulsion for the walls and eggshell for woodwork, sit flat against a surface and are less distracting and imposing on the eye.

There is an increasing range of finishes and colours now available in environmentally friendly paints. The essential difference is that these contain naturally occurring plant and vegetable oils, as opposed to petrochemicals. Of course, you can also take this one step further and mix your own paints using natural binders such as linseed oil tinted with pigment, or create traditional finishes such as limewash or distemper, which lend a softer, more organic appearance to walls.

Once you can see how the wall colour is going to look, you can start comparing swatches of flooring and fabrics from your storyboard against it and making your final decision about these.

Natural materials are always a good choice for the Zen home, but natural does not always mean environmentally friendly. Although it is not possible to completely avoid all products with chemical sealants or finishes there are a few simple things we can do. Check that wood and wood alternatives such as rattan and bamboo come from managed sources, and try to use natural wood stains and varnishes such as Shellac or linseed oil. When sourcing bed linen and cushion covers be aware of those with labels such as 'easy care' and 'non-iron', which will have been treated in some way for the 'benefit' of the consumer. Have a go at dyeing plain cottons and linens yourself with natural plant and vegetable dyes.

New life for old

Few of us are lucky enough to start every scheme from scratch and most of our ideas must also incorporate existing items into our plan. Part of planning our ideas is to consider how we can adapt items we cannot discard to fit into our overall vision. Kitchen units, for example, can have a style reinvention by painting each unit with a colour that matches the surrounding scheme, and changing the handles to create a more streamlined style. If the budget allows, you could also consider removing the door and drawer fronts and replacing them with plain pieces of wood, finished with a coat of paint if you prefer.

You can treat wooden furniture in the same way – strip an old and faded piece back to the bare wood and paint it to bring out the grain or replenish the colour of the wood itself, or use a coat of natural varnish such as Shellac to gently enhance the grain. It might be possible to alter the appearance of furniture by removing some of the decorative detail or again, changing door fronts or handles to spruce up the style.

Upholstered furniture can be given a new lease of life with different covers – inexpensive calico will work well against the pale backdrop of the Zen home and as a practical consideration, can be machine washed if spillage occurs. Likewise, simple pieces of furniture, such as wooden chairs or canvas director's chairs can be given a different look with simple white loose covers. (See pages 138-139 for details).

LEFT: Cupboard doors can be given a quick facelift with eye-catching handles to bring them into your new design scheme.

Loose chair cover

Give simple chairs a new streamlined look with loose-fitting cotton covers.
The following instructions can be adapted to fit any square chair with arms.

YOU WILL NEED:
- **Plain white cotton furnishing fabric 150cm/4ft 8in wide by length of your chair from floor at back to floor at front plus length of side panels (from top of arm to floor)**
- **Sewing kit and sewing machine**
- **Reel of white cotton thread**
- **Iron**

1 Take the following measurements from your chair (these will form the separate pieces for the cover) adding on 1cm/^{1}/$_2$in all around for seams plus 3cm/1^1/$_4$in at the lower edge for the hem. Measurements should be liberal (a couple of centimetres/inches bigger rather than smaller) so that the cover will slip easily over the chair.

2 Cut out pieces of fabric for the chair cover, marking each piece clearly so you can identify which piece goes where. With wrong sides facing, pin the main pieces of the chair cover together – back, seat and inner side arm pieces – over the chair. Machine along the seams, and press the seams open.

3 Place the stitched section of cover back over the chair, wrong side out, and pin further sections in place. Remove and machine stitch in place and then press the seams open. Continue in this way until all the pieces for the cover have been joined together (check that the chair cover fits comfortably as you go; where necessary take a little more or less seam allowance). Remove the cover from the chair. Turn the lower edge of cover over 1cm/^{1}/$_2$in to the wrong side and press. Now hem the bottom of the chair cover to the wrong side 3cm/1^1/$_4$in and pin in place – return the cover to the chair to check that the hem is level. Machine stitch or hand sew in place.

4 Trim the seam allowances and snip the seam turnings at the corners of the chair cover. Turn right side out and press.

A From floor at back, to base of back rest x width of back
B Base of seat back, across seat and down front to floor x width of seat
C Inside arm panel, from seat to top of arm x length from back rest to front of arm (2 pieces)
D Outer side panel, from floor to top of arm x length from back of chair to front (2 pieces)
E Gusset for side of back rest, from top of back rest to arm x 4cm/1^1/$_2$in
F Arm rest gusset, from top of arm at back rest to floor at front x 6cm/2^1/$_2$in

picture
credits

All project photography and the photographs on pages 1, 13 (bottom), 27 (bottom), 45, 57, 60-61, 63, 82, 94 (top left), 95 (top), 102-103, 106, 107 (top & right), 108, 112 (top), 133, 134, 135, were taken specially for the book by Peter Aprahamian.

Other photography reproduced by kind permission:
Livingetc (listed by photographer): 44 Photography, 58 (left); Graham Atkins Hughes, 12, 25 (bottom left), 85, 97 (top right), 111 (top right); Peter Aprahamian, 16-17, 20 (bottom left & right), 21, 22, 23, 30-31, 34 (top & bottom right), 35 (bottom right), 37, 39 (left), 56, 58 (right), 69, 70 (bottom left), 71, 78-79, 86, 87 (right), 95 (bottom right), 98 (right), 123, 128-129, 137 (bottom & far right); David Barrett, 2-3, 27 (left), 81 (top & bottom), 93 (top right & bottom left), 120 (top & bottom); Craig Knowles, 119; Tom Leighton, 15, 26, 27 (top right), 47 (top), 62, 83 (bottom left), 92, 97 (bottom), 98 (left), 121, 125 (right), 130; Hannah Lewis, 14, 94 (bottom right), 104, 109, 112 (bottom right), 136; David Loftus, 4-5, 54-55, 96, 105; Neil Mersch, 48, 49, 59, 74 (right), 111 (bottom right), 113; Jonathan Pilkington, 11, 50 (bottom right), 73, 111 (left), 122 (bottom); Ed Reeve, 25 (top), 50 (top right), 51 (right), 72; Trevor Richards, 124; Thomas Stewart; 34 (bottom left), 42-43, 50 (left), 68, 90-91, 99, 110, 116-117; Pia Tryde, 9, 44, 46; Chris Tubbs, 13 (top), 18, 66-67, 75, 83 (right), 87, 118, 122 (top), 137 (top left); Verity Welstead, 25 (bottom right), 35 (top), 47 (bottom), 51 (left); Henry Wilson, 32; Polly Wreford, 38 (top & bottom), 39 (right), 125 (left); Mel Yates. p93 (bottom right).

Peter Aprahamian, pp6-7, 36, 70 (top), 80.

Matthew Priestman, p24 (photographer Peter Aprahamian).

Many thanks go to the following companies for supplying items used in the original photography of this book.

Anne Musso, 4 Great Western Studios, Great Western Rd, London, W9 (0171 266 1776 for stockists), for the hand thrown bottles and bowls, 10 & 41, and the hand thrown porcelain bowl, 61.

Burlington Slate, 01229 889 661 (for stockists).

Conran Collection, 12 Conduit Street, London, W1, for the wooden bowl, 57 (bottom left), small wooden bowl, 74 (left) & 77, and wicker box and cushion, 139.

Egg, 36 Kinnerton Street, London, SW1, for the silk shawl, 10, tall vases, 13 (bottom), silk cushions, 57 (bottom right), large round bowl, 95 (top), small bowls, 106 (top left), and felt slippers, 139.

Interiors Bis, 60 Sloane Ave, London SW3, for the white armchair and console table, 13, and console table, 41.

Purves & Purves, 80-81 Tottenham Court Road, London, W1, for the wicker chair, 63 (top), 65 & 82, wooden side table, 74 (left) & 77.

Also, a big thank you to Mette Johnson, picture editor at *Livingetc*, for her patience and help with picture research for this book.

project index

index

First published in 1999 by Ward Lock
Illustrated Division
The Orion Publishing Group
Wellington House
125 Strand
London WC2R 0BB

Livingetc is published eleven times per year by IPC
Magazines Limited, Kings Reach Tower, Stamford Street,
London SE1 9LS. For subscription enquiries and orders
please call 01444 445555 (fax no: 01444 445599). For credit
card orders call the subscription credit card hotline
(UK orders only) on 01622 778778.

ISBN: 0 70637 869 5

Series Editor: Ljiljana Ortolja-Baird
Editor: Alison Moss
Text Editor: Nikoletta Stamatatos
Designer: Bet Ayer
Projects Photographer: Peter Aprahamian
Projects Stylist: Jane Tidbury